JAMES JOYCE IN OSTEND

XAVIER TRICOT

JAMES JOYCE IN OSTEND

Second revised and expanded edition

PANDORA PUBLISHERS

For their invaluable help and the provision of crucial information, I would like to thank the staff of the National Library of Ireland, Dublin; the James Joyce Centre, Dublin; the James Joyce Foundation, Zurich; the Huntington Library, San Marino, California; the Valery Larbaud Archives, Médiathèque Valery Larbaud, Vichy, France; and the Division of Rare and Manuscript Collections, Cornell University Library, Ithaca, New York. I am especially grateful to James Maynard, Curator of the Poetry Collection at the University Libraries, University at Buffalo, the State University of New York. I also extend my thanks to Helen Simpson for her critical reading and remarks.

Heureux qui, comme Ulysse, a fait un beau voyage…

Joachim du Bellay (1522-1560)

Seeking respite from the summer heat of Paris, James Joyce arrived in Ostend on 5 or 6 August 1926. He was accompanied by his wife Nora and daughter Lucia. In a letter dated 25 July 1926 to Harriet Shaw Weaver (1876-1961), the British activist and editor of the magazine *The Egoist*, Joyce writes:

> […] *It is far too hot and the franc having fallen to 250 has jumped back to 192 in four days and tomorrow is my daughter's birthday (19) and on the next day my son comes of age and Miss Beach has gone to S. Patrick's birthplace, Boulogne, and I am thinking of going to Ostend.* […][1]

In his letter, Joyce makes reference to his daughter Lucia, born in Trieste on 26 July 1907 and his son Giorgio (later named George), born in the same city on 27 June 1905. He also refers to Sylvia Beach (1887-1962), an American bibliophile, whom he had met in Paris in 1920. Beach was the founder and proprietor of the bookshop Shakespeare & Co., which had opened its doors at 8 rue Dupuytren in November 1919. She has moved her shop to 12 rue de l'Odéon in 1921. Shakespeare & Co. was a nexus for book-lovers and authors, a place where people exchanged ideas and where Sylvia Beach introduced writers to publishers. Her decision to publish Joyce's *Ulysses* in 1922, at a time when no other British or American publisher would touch the manuscript for fear of censorship, had made her bookshop famous.

It is not known why Joyce selected Ostend as his summer refuge. Popular since the turn of the century, the Belgian coastal town was a magnet for the European *beau monde* and other assorted rich and famous characters. Some of the greatest stars of the day performed in the plays, concerts, recitals and operas that were staged at the Casino and Théâtre Royal. Others were drawn to the horse races at the Wellington

Hippodrome. The luxury hotels along the promenade were often fully booked. By all accounts, the season of 1926 was a glittering success. The Shah of Persia, Ahmed Qajar (1898-1930), and the Indian Maharajah of Baruda, Gaekwad III (1863-1939), were guests of the Royal Palace Hotel during the early weeks of August. They could have expected to see Russian ballet dancers at the Casino, or the Italian pianist Gualtiero Volterra (1901-1967), the Italian opera singer Pasquale Amato (1878-1942) and the French violinist Gabriel Bouillon (1898-1984). The Spanish soprano Elvira de Hidalgo (1888-1980), who later taught Maria Callas (1923-1977), was married to the manager of the establishment and a regular performer. Verdi's *Rigoletto*, Puccini's *La Tosca* and *Paillasse* by Leoncavallo were all staged at the Théâtre Royal. This was also the year of Ostend's first important international air rally, which was held from 26 to 28 June 1926. Around fifteen aeroplanes competed, including the RSV O-BADA, piloted by the Belgian aviator Jean Stampe (1889-1978), and two Handley Page W.8 models, the O-BAHU and O-BAHL. The Belgian airline, Sabena, had introduced the latter planes into its fleet just a month earlier. Their British designer, Frederick Handley Page (1885-1962), also attended the rally, as did the Belgian aviator Georges Medaets (1896-1976). Medaets landed his Breguet 19 in Ostend, the same plane that he had recently piloted to and from the Congo.

The Sunday issue of the local newspaper *La Saison d'Ostende et du Littoral*, dated 8 August 1926, stressed the *couleur locale* in an article that was published in English:

> British visitors to Ostend. Cross-channel boat crowded.
> On the first Monday in August, bank-holiday, large numbers of British visitors come to Ostende [*sic*], others go to Zeebrugge and Antwerp, all the boats being filled at their utmost capacity. The rush this year began on the Thursday before the holiday and trains were overcrowded, boats doubled. It is sometime a matter for speculation where all this crowd is accommodated [*sic*], as although the entire Belgian coast from La Panne to the Le Zoute is a succession of white, palatial hotels, of smiling villas, even these have their limit of accommodation [*sic*] and rooms are not elastic. In any case, the people were all put up somewhere and are apparently contented with the accommodation [*sic*], as what they really want, is a breath of sea-air, in a place where

they can always count on fair weather, for even if there are showers, they do not last. The sandy soil dries almost immediately. The sand dunes, too, that form a wonderful playground for the children, dry within a few minutes, making Ostend and the Belgian coast generally a wonderful place for small people.

This week there are all kinds of competitions for sand castles, for which the beach is very suitable, while the Ostend sand lends itself most specially to the work of building, modelling and manipulation generally, as it dries very quickly and is sufficiently consistent to keep the shape given it, a great advantage for the sculptors. While the children construct wonderful models, think out all kinds of curious ideas to be carried out in sand, the grown-ups sometimes give them a hand. It is well worth while walking along the beach at Ostend, especially towards Mariakerke, somewhat away from the great throng, to look at some of the works of art done in sand. Sculptors, on holidays, will try their hand on the new material, with somewhat starling results and as the creator of the wonderful model does not give away the secret that he is a professional, people passing by wonder at the skill of the children.

Ostend beach is gay with all kinds of colours at this time of year. Of a morning the bathers come down to the beach in all kinds of bright-coloured dresses, and the British visitors, considering that the clothes they bring with them look dull among the bright colours, frequently buy something ready-made to put on of a morning. They get something still more bright and gay for their children, and this gives colour to the beach. The bathers wear red and blue gowns, but it is rare that the type of bathing-dress seen at Deauville or Dieppe is worn at Ostend. […]

The picture gallery in the Kursaal, with its works of West-Flemish painters, attract many visitors, the British especially have always been keen of the Dutch and the Flemish schools, and it is probably that purchases will be made of pictures that will be carried away to country houses in England and the States.

Wellington Race course is a mass of colour this year, as usual. Perhaps the colours are a triffle [sic] more vivid, the jewellery worn by the ladies a bit brighter and prettier than usual. Breedene [sic], the course where serious racing men concregate [sic], is also crowded, but owing to the distance from Ostend, there are fewer women and a preponderance of men among the habitual racing-crowd.[2]

On 22 August 1926, Ostend was also mentioned in *The New York Times*:

OSTEND, Aug. 21. -- Here in this most fashionable of Belgian Summer resorts one sees the microcosm of Europe at play. It is playing so whole-heartedly and even so merrily that one might forget that beyond this ornamental promenade, with its row of palatial hotels on one side and stretch of firm white sands on the other, there exists another and larger Europe, where the things that matter have a very different aspect.

Upon their arrival in the city, James, Nora and Lucia Joyce initially stayed at the Littoral Palace, situated on the corner of the Hertstraat and the Promenade. On 6 August, Joyce sent a postcard to Sylvia Beach:

[Picture Postcard]
N.D. Postmark: 6 August 1926   *Ostende*

Greetings from here. By chance we stopped at the Auberge Littoral Palace A.L.P. but leave on Monday for some place cheaper. Add: Poste Restante.

Kindest regards
J.J.[3]

For Joyce, the initials of the Auberge Littoral Palace in Ostend corresponded with those of Anna Livia Plurabelle, the female protagonist of *Work in Progress*, which he had commenced in 1923 and was then still writing. In reality, the hotel was simply called the Littoral Palace, with Joyce adding 'Auberge' of his own accord. By 1926, Joyce had already published extracts of *Work in Progress* in the Parisian literary magazines *Transatlantic Review, Transition* and *Le Navire d'argent.* This is the book that he would eventually publish in 1939 as *Finnegans Wake* (Faber and Faber, London and the Viking Press, New York). Joyce concluded his postcard with news of the family's impending move to a cheaper hotel. On 9 August 1926, the Joyce family moved to the Hôtel du Phare, also situated on the Promenade, although closer to the harbour.

The following day, Joyce sent Sylvia Beach another postcard, dated 10 August:

[Picture Postcard]
10 August 1926   *Hôtel du Phare, Ostende, Belgium*

Dear Miss Beach: You see where I am now but we shall have to change again so my address will better be P.R. [Poste Restante] here. I like it very much but is very crowded and dreadfully dear. I hope you are both well. ∧ is here. When I arrived I walked into a pharmacy to buy ouate [cotton wool]. *The chemist said: Are you J.J.? I said: I am. He said: I'm Pat Hoey from Dublin. Hoey and Joyce are the same name. I knew him 25 years ago.*

> *Kindest regards*
> *J.J.*
> *Nora Joyce* [4]

The inverted triangle in the message is a symbol (or siglum) for Shaun in *Finnegans Wake*, Joyce's unorthodox chronicle of the Earwicker family: Humphrey Chimpden Earwicker, the patriarch, his wife Anna Livia Plurabelle, and their three children Kevin (Shaun), Jerry (Shem) and Isabel. [5] Joyce goes on to mention that he has met a fellow Irishman named Patrick Hoey in Ostend, whom he identifies *a posteriori* with Shaun (siglum: inverted triangle), or with a 'prototype' of Shaun.

Little is known about Patrick Hoey and his relationship with Joyce. One would expect to find Hoey's name in the 1926 register of foreign nationals residing in Ostend, together with vital data, but there is no trace of him in the local archives, many of which were destroyed when the Germans bombed the city in May 1940. What can be ascertained, however, is that Patrick Hoey worked as a chemist's assistant at the *Pharmacie anglaise* (English Pharmacy) on the corner of the Adolf Buylstraat and the Marie-Joséplein in Ostend, which was owned by Albert Bouchery (1858-1941). First located in the Kaaistraat, it moved to the Adolf Buylstraat in 1898 before being integrated into the new 'Bouchery' apartment building that was built on the Marie-Joséplein in 1911. Albert Bouchery was also the founder, publisher and editor (until 1923) of the local newspaper *Le Carillon*.[6] What brought Patrick Hoey to Ostend is a matter of conjecture, as is the date of his arrival and the circumstances of his employment in a local chemist's shop.

The James Joyce Collection at the University of New York in Buffalo contains one of Patrick Hoey's calling cards, which appears to have been sent to Sylvia Beach at the end of August 1926, together with a set of photographs that were principally taken by Lucia Joyce. On one of these photographs, we see James and Nora Joyce with Patrick Hoey, reclining on the grass (see Album of photographs, plate X).

The calling card is printed with the following details:

P. J. Hoey
334, N.C.R.
Phibsboro
Dublin

The abbreviation 'N.C.R.' stands for 'North Circular Road', a street in the mixed commercial and residential neighbourhood of Phibsborough in Dublin, Ireland (alternative spelling: Phibsboro). This is where Patrick Hoey was domiciled during his stay in Ostend. Joyce had also been a resident of Phibsborough during his early twenties, living first on Glengarriff Parade and then on St. Peter's Terrace.

But who was Patrick J. Hoey and what do we know of his life? Hoey is a common Irish surname, and the forename Patrick is even more ubiquitous. Joyce expands on his friendship with his compatriot in a subsequent letter to Harriet Shaw Weaver, which he wrote in Ostend on 18 August 1926:

> *Mr Patrick Hoey whom I met here behind a chemist's counter recognised me after an interval of 24 years. He was present at a supper given me before I went to Paris in 1902. He is a great admirer of my works and pomps and has all the first editions. He is in fact a very good Λ all the more as his name is the same as my own. Joyeux, Joyes, Joyce (Irish Sheehy or Hoey, the Irish change J into Sh e.g. James Sheumas, John Shaun etc). He very often uses the identical words I put into Λ's mouth at the Euclid lesson before coming down here.[7]*

12

This particular letter is crucial in terms of providing a positive identification for the man in question. The Irish census records for 1911 (compiled on 2 April) provide details of a certain Patrick J. Hoey: his occupation is a chemist, he is single, 36 years old, born in County Louth and resides at 43 Belvedere Place, Dublin. From this we can deduce that he was born in 1875. Trying to establish his parentage, however, is more complicated. In 1875, two children were born in Drogheda, County Louth, both called Patrick Hoey. One was baptised on 2 June 1875, the son of William Hoey and Mary Anne Bannon; the other was baptised on 23 May 1875, the son of Patrick Hoey and Elizabeth Murphy. A third Patrick Hoey was born in Tallanstown, County Louth, and baptised on 8 January 1875, the son of John Hoey and Bridget Sweeney.[8] It is impossible to know which one of these children ultimately befriended Joyce.

Returning to the census of 1911, a widow named Mary O'Brien and her two sons, Daniel and William O'Brien, are listed at the same address: 43 Belvedere Place, Dublin. William O'Brien (1881-1968), then working as a tailor, went on to become the famous Irish socialist and republican, editor, trade union leader and Dáil deputy. It seems that Patrick Hoey and William O'Brien were not just neighbours but also friends. The National Library of Ireland (Dublin) contains a photographic postcard that Hoey sent to O'Brien from Brussels.[9] Dated 23 September 1910, the envelope bears the following address: *Mr. W. O'Brien / 43 Belvedere Place / Dublin, / Ireland*. On the front of the card is an image pertaining to the execution on 13 October 1909 of Francisco Ferrer (1859-1909), a Spanish pedagogue and libertarian anarchist. The case was an international *cause célèbre*. Hoey writes:

> *I thought this would suit you – that's why I'm sending it. It's the demonstration around the Ferrar* [sic] *execution.*

Was Patrick Hoey in Brussels during the first Pan-Celtic Congress that was held on 24-31 August 1910? This was an initiative of the *Union Celtique* (Celtic Union), which had been established by a group of Brussels-based Irishmen in November 1908. Yet Patrick Hoey is not mentioned in the list of members assisting at the Congress, the proceedings of which were published in the special 1911 edition of the *Bulletin de l'Union Celtique* (*The Pan Celtic Quarterly*).

The National Library of Ireland also owns a copy of *Les Gens de Dublin*, with a dedication from Joyce on the title page: *'To Patrick Hoey | James Joyce'.*[10] Unfortunately, there is no mention of the place and date. *Les Gens de Dublin* is the French translation of *The Dubliners*, which was published in April 1926 by Plon-Nourrit & Co., Paris. Was this edition despatched from Shakespeare & Co. to Patrick Hoey in Ostend? Or did Joyce bring copies of *Les Gens de Dublin* with him to Belgium? The provenance of the book held by the National Library of Ireland is unknown.[11] On 14 August 1926, Patrick Hoey sent a letter from Ostend to Shakespeare & Co.:

[printed heading]

PHARMACIE ANGLAISE Ostende, le *14th August 1926*
    A. BOUCHERY Téléphone 1111
PHARMACIEN DE LA COUR
CHEMIST TO THE COUR [*sic*]
7, SQUARE MARIE-JOSÉ

Pharmaciens { Alb. Bouchery
              Alfred Paulus

Dear Sirs

    Mr James Joyce – a very old friend of mine gave me | a copy of his book 'Ulysses' a few days ago. It is fully twenty | years ago since I saw him last. He is now staying in Ostende | for the season. He told me that if I wanted to have the book | autographed by him it would be necessary to obtain | your permission – and he thought that if I wrote and told you | the circumstances you would not withhold it. Trusting | you may see your way to give the necessary leave and hoping | to have a line or two from you at your convenience

I remain
   Your faithfully
      Patrick Hoey.

Shakespeare and Company.
   12 Rue de l'Odéon
      Paris.

Myrsine Moschos, Sylvia Beach's assistant, pencilled the following note on the envelope:

Please excuse me | Mr. J. Joyce having us to send book to this address | I thought that his friend was ordering also some books from us I opened this letter.

Myrsine[12]

In his letter to Shakespeare & Co., Patrick Hoey mentions that Joyce presented him with a copy of *Ulysses* 'a few days ago'. Since the letter was written on 14 August, we can assume that he met the writer around 10 August, which corresponds with the content of the postcard that Joyce sent to Sylvia Beach on 10 August 1926 (cf. *supra*).

On 11 August, Joyce sent a postcard to Harriet Shaw Weaver:

Ostende 11/VIII/26

Dear Miss Weaver: We have been | here a few days and are busy enjoying | the good air and food and hotel hunting. | When I have more a good caterer [?] *| I will write my official report | post ordered* [?] *pour Paris. This is by | far the best place we have been | in for a summer holiday – sauf bonne fin! I hope you are well | and also Mrs. Marsden.* [a small oval] = [illegible word] | *companions.* [a small rectangle] = [illegible word or abbreviation; perhaps 'section' or 'chapter'] *12.* [an inverted T] = *Tristan | form* [or from?] *10 I had to change here to* [symbol?] *| With kindest regards | Sincerely yours| James Joyce.*[13]

By all accounts, the author was enjoying his stay in Ostend but, nevertheless, was still 'hotel hunting'. Joyce mentions Dora Marsden (1882-1960), an English suffragette, editor of literary journals, and philosopher of language. She was the publisher of suffragist magazine, *Freewoman*, which eventually became *The New Freewoman*. The magazine was renamed *The Egoist* in 1914, and Weaver succeeded Marsden as editor. Through the involvement of Ezra Pound, the publication became associated with modernist literature and published avant-garde writers such as Joyce, T. S. Eliot (1888-1965) and Percy Wyndham Lewis (1882-1957), who was also a well-known painter. The message ends with a number of symbols, including an oval, rectangle and an inverted T. [14] Joyce identifies the figure of Tristan with an inverted T, although this symbol was normally assigned to Isolde within the system. In this, the writer was inspired by Wagner's *Tristan and Isolde* and *Le Roman de Tristan et Iseult* by the French scholar Joseph Bédier (1864-1938). [15]

In his next letter to Harriet Shaw Weaver, dated Wednesday 18 August (cited above), Joyce writes:

Hôtel de l'Océan, Digue de Mer, Ostende

Dear Miss Weaver: The map in the papers does not show your part of England as affected so I hope you did not feel any shock the other morning. We were awake all night nearly on Monday but the worst of the storm was in London. Jeeshee and Kami-nari are very active just now. Miss Beach writes from Les Déserts (Savoy) that the house next to hers was struck. Why do they go there? I wish they were back and the tiresome badtempered [sic] *summer over. I am by no means ascetic here for I have developed a most Flemish appetite which I trust will not always abide with me. Yesterday I ran from Middelkerke to Mariakerke, a distance of about 6 or 7 kilometres. I could walk for ever along a strand.*

There is some news. Mr Roth has now turned Two Worlds *into a monthly and is publishing* Ulysses *in it. The July number contained the whole* Telemachia. *We do not know what to do. The editor of the* New York Herald Tribune *writes to Miss Beach asking if Mr Roth is authorised to do this and offers to intervene. The number is dedicated to me with profound admiration or something like that! O dear!*

There is no news yet from The Dial. *Mr Patrick Hoey whom I met here behind a chemist's counter recognised me after an interval of 24 years. He was present at a supper given me before I went to Paris in 1902. He is a great admirer of my works and pomps and has all the first editions. He is in fact a very good ∧ all the more as his name is the same as my own. Joyeux, Joyes, Joyce (Irish Sheehy or Hoey, the Irish change J into Sh e.g. James Sheumas, John Shaun etc). He very often uses the identical words I put into ∧'s mouth at the Euclid lesson before coming down here.*

If you ever put on my disk I would be much obliged if you or Miss Marsden would note the points of the Irish brogue in it, chiefly on the consonants. I asked Mrs Pound to do so but she may forget it. This would be

Two lighthouses and Cercle du Phare, later Hôtel royal du Phare, c. 1910.

Seafront Promenade, Hôtel Littoral Palace (white building, center of the photo), Ostend, c. 1910.

Seafront Promenade, Hôtel de l'Océan, Ostend, c. 1910.

Sea baths, Ostend, c. 1910.

175. **Ostende** Rampe de Flandre et B^d Van Iseghem **Ostend**

Corner Rue de Flandre and Boulevard Van Iseghem, Ostend, c.1920.

Saints Peter and Paul Church, Ostend, c. 1925

Ostende. — Entrée de la rue de la Chapelle

Entrance Chapel Street, Ostend, c. 1925.

Ostende   La place d'Armes et l'Hôtel de Ville.

Main Square and Town Hall, Ostend, c. 1925.

very useful to me though I did not speak it in my natural voice.
  With kindest regards to Miss Marsden and yourself and hopes for your her
and my quiet of mind.[16]

Joyce makes reference to the heavy thunderstorm that blew into Ostend on Monday 16 August. The words 'Jeeshee' and 'Kami-nari' are typical Joycean 'bastardisations' of the Japanese words *jishin*, which means thunder, and *kamikari* which means earthquake.[17] Joyce also tells Weaver about the events of the previous day (Tuesday 17 August), namely his walk along the beach from Middelkerke (a small coastal town at about 9 kilometres from Ostend, towards De Panne, near the French boarder) to Mariakerke (a former village on the outskirts of Ostend with a picturesque church, Our-Lady-of-the-Dunes). The churchyard also contains the grave of the celebrated Ostend painter, James Ensor (1860-1949), who was buried there on 23 November 1949.

Joyce is bothered about Samuel Roth (1893-1974), an American publisher who, in the mid-1920s, used the profits from his language school for immigrants to establish a number of literary journals. The most important titles in his short-lived magazine empire were the quarterly *Two Worlds* and *Two Worlds Monthly*. He chose to publish, in some cases without permission, works by some of the most sexually explicit contemporary writers, including excerpts of James Joyce's *Ulysses* (which appeared in *Two Worlds Monthly*). Joyce won an injunction to stop Roth from printing these expurgated texts. At the writer's behest, Sylvia Beach spearheaded an international protest against Roth in 1927, although the nature of copyright law at the time made it difficult to prove the charge of piracy. As a result of this well-organised outcry by a total of some 167 authors, Roth became an international literary pariah and Random House won its case to publish the unexpurgated text of *Ulysses* in 1934. Not long afterwards, Roth produced unauthorised editions of *Lady Chatterley's Lover*, almost certainly the first American to take the risk. After a raid on his Fifth Avenue warehouse by the New York Society for the Suppression of Vice in 1929, Roth spent over a year in prison on Welfare Island, as well as in Philadelphia, on charges of distributing pornography.[18]

In early July 1926, Joyce offered the 'Shaun' episodes from *Work in Progress* to *The Dial*, a long-running and prestigious American review that was run by the poet Scofield Thayer (1889-1982). Having initially accepted the text, the editors cabled Joyce to ask for a number of deletions before finally rejecting the work. Joyce had been working on the 'Shaun' episodes (which later became Book III of *Finnegans Wake*) since March 1924. While other parts of *Work in Progress* had been published by Samuel Roth in *Two Worlds*, the 'Shaun' passages had yet to see the light of day.

Joyce was keen to find a prestigious American publication in which he could serialise his work on a regular basis. The London correspondent for *The Dial* was none other than the poet T. S. Eliot, one of Thayer's friends. In November 1922, *The Dial* had published Eliot's poem *The Waste Land*, thereby introducing the work to an American audience for the first time, while '*Ulysses*, Order and Myth', an important essay on *Ulysses* by Eliot, was published in November 1923 (vol. LXXV, no. 5, pp. 480-483). *The Dial* had sent Joyce a telegram to confirm the rate of a halfpenny per word, with a note stating that the editors would review the text beforehand. Joyce had posted the manuscript on 25 July, and in a letter written to Harriet Weaver that same day, described himself as feeling like a debutante at her first coming-out. *The Dial* did not respond until September. As Joyce explained in a subsequent letter to Harriet Weaver, he was initially offered a fee of $600 dollars for the piece. A week later, he received another telegram to say that 'Shaun' could not be printed in its current form. Not wishing to make any cuts to the text, Joyce told Weaver that he had decided to withdraw his submission. He was aggrieved, not least because *The Dial* was a prestigious publication, but also because he feared that such a rejection might spoil his chances of publishing the work elsewhere. In a letter written a few days later, Joyce explained that *The Dial* had wanted to cut a third of the text, which he found unacceptable. Versions of the 'Shaun' episodes were published for the first time in *Transition* as of March 1928.[19]

In this same letter, Joyce also refers to Patrick Hoey and remarks that he owns all of his first editions. Hoey had also attended Joyce's farewell dinner on 4 November 1902 at the Nassau Hotel, South Frederick Street, Dublin. Organised by the Irish poet William Butler Yeats (1865-1939), it preceded Joyce's departure for Paris. Lady Augusta Isabella Gregory (1852-1932), the Irish playwright, poet and co-founder of the Irish Literary Theatre and Abbey Theatre, was also a guest. Patrick Hoey was an acquaintance, therefore, of both Joyce and Yeats, the latter of whom wrote him several letters between 1908 and 1909.[20]

The 'Euclid Lesson', which Joyce also mentions, was part of *Work in Progress* (and also included in *Finnegans Wake*). At the end of his letter, Joyce makes reference to his 'disk', which is the 1924 recording of the 'Aeolus' episode in *Ulysses* that was made at His Master's Voice studios at Billancourt, near Paris.

In addition to other family members (named as Owen Hoey and Annie Hoey), Joyce lists Patrick Hoey as a character in one of his notebooks (a cheap copybook that belonged to his sister Mabel) alongside notes for one of the (ultimately lost) chapters of his novel *Stephen Hero*.[21] On the subject of Irish people named Hoey, the Joycean scholar Tim Finnegan writes about these fictional characters in his blog, 'An annotated Stephen Hero':

> The next set of names clearly refers mostly to later, University chapters, but some Belvedere hints may have slipped in:
>
> | | |
> |---|---|
> | Fr Webster | [Darlington, changed to 'Butt'] |
> | Fr Dillon | [UC president Delany] |
> | Miles Davin | [Clancy, changed to 'Madden'] |
> | James Brennan | [Byrne?, changed to 'Cranly' if so] Matthew Lister [Thomas Lyster?] |
> | Thomas Nash Oliver Flanagan | |
> | | [Gogarty, mentioned briefly at TS225] |
> | Patrick Hoey | |
> | Owen Hoey | |
> | Annie Hoey[22] | |

In a list of subscribers for a new parish church in Louth, drawn up in 1890, we find the following names:

Mrs. Hoey, Annagassan, 10/-, [Dunleer]
Mrs. Hoey, Corballis, £1, [Cooley]
Mr. John Hoey, Reaghstown, £1, [Cooley]
Mr. Owen Hoey, Drumgoolin, £2, [Louth]
Mr. Pat Hoey, Drumgoolin, £2, [Louth]
Mr. Patrick Hoey, Oaktate, 10/-, [Louth][23]

The Joycean scholars Vincent Deane, Daniel Ferrer and Geert Lernout, have published and analysed the author's famous Notebooks.[24] Furthermore, Lernout has also uncovered some interesting notes and findings written by Joyce in relation to his encounters in Ostend:

References to things Belgian in notebook VI.B.12 start on page 100 ('suikerstuck' [piece of sugar]), but the earliest entries that can be attributed with some degree of certainty to the Belgian holiday (and not to the reading of guidebooks) are four references to Patrick Hoey, an old Dublin acquaintance whom we know Joyce met in a pharmacy the day he arrived in Ostend. On a postcard to Sylvia Beach and in a letter to Harriet Weaver, Joyce described Hoey as a Shaun figure: 'He is in fact a very good [??].... He very often uses the identical words I put into [??]'s mouth at the Euclid lesson before coming down here' (LI: 244). The speech of the boys in the first drafts of section 8 of II.2 are indeed marked by a Dublin brogue.

Notebook VI.B.12 has four references to Hoey. The first is a puzzling 'Hoey dillidantis' on page 164, and the last on page 178 is surely ironic: 'Hoey - I haven't much of a brogue.' Between them are two expressions that made it into *Finnegans Wake*. 'Hoey - sure you'd write as good as that yrself. Pat' was first heavily Dublinised and then, with a number of French and Flemish words, almost immediately introduced into the fair copy of the geometry lesson as '(Sure, you could rite as foyne as that yerself, mick!)' (BL 47478 f. 11; JJA 53: 42). The second was destined for the 'Musey-room' scene in chapter 1: 'Hoey-Mind yr boot going out.'

That Joyce was still using this notebook at the end of August is clear from a reference on page 186 to 'Pas sur la bouche (Just a Kiss),' an apparently rather risqué operetta that played at the Théâtre de la Scala in Ostend at the beginning of September. In addition, at the end of the notebook (and starting on page 187) there are several references to Ghent, the city to which Joyce and his family moved to on 13 September, although these notes might have been made earlier, in preparation for the move, from a guidebook such as the *Gand guide illustré*, the title of which occurs in the following notebook.[25]

Joyce states that his own surname and that of Hoey have the same etymological roots, which leads us to surmise that his brush with Patrick Hoey in Ostend was far from insignificant. It was undoubtedly a chance meeting, although Joyce may well have seen it as a stroke of luck. Could he have viewed the encounter as a kind of 'epiphany'? Did Joyce view Patrick Hoey as a kind of avatar as a result of their common etymological heritage?

In a letter written at the end August or 1 September 1932, sent from Feldkirch (Austria) to his Irish friend Alfred Bergan (1887-1941) in Dublin, Joyce once again mentions Patrick Hoey:

Hotel zum Löwen, Feldkirch

Dear Mr Bergan, Thanks very much for your letter. I return you, as you wish, the catalogues. I prefer Design No. 120 which is the simplest, and enclose the inscription. Will Messrs. Harrison please let me know the total cost, and also when the headstone can be erected, and the manner and time of payment which they desire?
I am staying here with my wife and daughter who, I am glad to say, is much better, but must return to Zurich in a week or so and then to Paris. But any letter sent me here will be forwarded.
I remember quite well Mr. Harding, and heard from our common friend Patrick Hoey in Ostend a few years ago a very amusing description of the attendance at his funeral.
I am very grateful for all the trouble you are taking on my behalf. Sincerely yours,

James Joyce

P.S. Would it be possible to have the whole done in white marble, gravestone and headstone, or is this for technical reason, or on account of some regulation in the cemetery, not advisable?[26]

According to a note to this letter, Patrick Hoey is 'a chemist's assistant who worked in Graham's Pharmacy in Westmoreland Street. He was a well-known man about town, good at after-dinner speaking and singing'.[27] Graham's Pharmacy was a well-known chemist's shop in the centre of Dublin. It closed its doors in 1975:

It was a pearl among pharmacies. It had been on the go since 1897. But in the summer of 1975, JJ Graham's on Westmoreland Street closed its doors for the last time. 'And now even Graham's is gone,' reads the somewhat exasperated headline on an elegiac story by Elgy Gillespie. Gillespie writes that the first sale in the pharmacy's prescription book was for a pomade for a client on Fitzwilliam Square, cost one shilling (which is akin to Creme de la Mer skin-care prices nowadays). Almond hand cream was made out of whole unpeeled almonds. Graham's also made its own toothpaste – from soap powder, camphor and precipitated chalk – while its famously foul-tasting hangover cure is revealed as 'a compound of bromivalarium and Alka Seltzer'[28]

The 'Mr Harding' referred to by Joyce was Patrick Harding, a solicitor in the Estate Duty Office of the Customs House, and a friend of Joyce's father.[29] Thanks to letters written by the Irish actor Frank Fay (1870-1931) to Patrick Hoey, located at the Huntington Library (San Marino, California), mostly sent while Fay was touring England and the USA with the 'Irish Players', we know more about Hoey's interest in Irish theatre and literature.[30] Frank Fay and his brother William (1872-1947) were the co-founders of the Abbey Theatre in Dublin. In its early years, the theatre was closely associated with the writers of the so-called Irish Literary Revival, the majority of whom were founding members and whose works formed part of the repertoire. Many of the great 20th-century Irish playwrights, including William Butler Yeats, Lady Gregory, Seán O'Casey (1880-1964) and John Millington Synge (1871-1909), premiered their plays at the Abbey Theatre, which were often performed by the finest actors of the day. Frank Fay seems to have been particularly close to Hoey.

In the letters that he wrote between 12 February 1906 and 6 December 1911, Fay provides detailed reports on the audience reactions to the Irish Players' productions. He also elaborates on the actors' performances, the work of the stage directors and about future plans and strategies. On a postcard, stamped 17 July 1907, Frank Fay even asks Patrick Hoey to write a small theatre piece, most probably a comedy or a skit:

P. Hoey Esq.
c/o Mess. Graham
Chemists
Westmoreland St.
Dublin

<del>Tuesday</del> Wednesday

Are you working at that little matter you wot [sic] *of? If not, will you try
your hand. Something small at first – say 30 minutes. Begin now, if you
have the idea, & take lots of time. But only do something you will thoroughly
enjoy doing, & and do it when you enjoy doing it. Best wishes F. J. F.*[31]

In undated letter (most probably from 1907), Fay adds in a post scriptum:
'What about that play you thought of writing of us?'[32] It is not known whether
Patrick Hoey followed up on Fay's suggestion. Curiously, Fay does not
send any of his letters to his friend's home address, Belvedere Place, but to
Graham's Pharmacy, Westmoreland Street, Dublin.

Joyce was well-acquainted with the Fay brothers. His biographer,
Richard Ellmann, relates the author's first encounter with the siblings on
the night of 20 June 1904:

> On this night he turned up at the rehearsal of the National Theatre
> Society, which was then meeting in a makeshift theatre, really a large
> storehouse behind a grocery shop in Camden Street. After closing-
> time, this back-room, later to be dignified as the Camden Hall, could
> only be reached through a long narrow passage dimly lit by a gas jet.
> Joyce's visits were usually tolerated by the actors because he would
> entertain them by singing in the breaks during rehearsal, and Holloway
> records that Joyce had been present ten days before when Synge
> announced to the society that he had a new play ready for them, The
> Well of the Saints. Synge's productivity probably encouraged Joyce to
> demonstrate splenetically his continued contempt for the Irish theater,
> for he arrived so drunk on June 20 that he collapsed in the passageway.
> Just then Vera Esposito, who was one of the actresses, came out with
> her mother; walking through the passage she stumbled over something
> and heard with astonishment its maudlin grunts. Hastily retreating

she informed Frank and William Fay, the company's directors, of the presence of the obstacle. They crowded in with candles and identified the prostrate form. After a slight scuffle Joyce was evicted and the door slammed and bolted behind him. [...] But soon as he recovered his wits he revenged himself by a poem:

> *O, there are two brothers, the Fays,*
> *Who are excellent players of plays,*
> *And, needless to mention, all*
> *Most unconventional,*
> *Filling the world with amaze.*
>
> *But I angered those brothers, the Fays,*
> *Whose ways are conventional ways,*
> *For I lay in my urine*
> *While the ladies so pure in*
> *White petticoats ravished my gaze.*[33]

Ironically, William Fay would later direct Joyce's play *Exiles* at the Regent Theatre in London, on 14 and 15 February 1926.[34]

On Thursday 24 August, Joyce wrote to Sylvia Beach:

24 August 1926   *Hôtel de l'Océan, Digue de Mer, Ostende*

Dear Miss Beach: I am returning your enclosures to me. Do not do anything till you return to Paris and till the Dial replies. I think we shall stay here till 1 or 2 prox and then go to Ghent for a few days. In any case we shall remain in Leopoldland [Belgium]. *I had a letter from Miss Weaver who is well but her sister's house was struck by lightning. I wish the summer was ygangen out as the old song ought to have sung. I send the N.L.* [Les Nouvelles littéraires] *to Miss Monnier. When she goes back to Paris she would oblige me if she withdraws Carducci's article from M.* [Mesures?] *and gives it to* La Revue [La Revue Nouvelle]. *I forget what it reviews but Mr Manoel Lelis* [Manuel-Lélis] *is the editor. I met him here a few days ago. I hope you are having a good holiday. You may write here as even if we leave I shall give them our next address.*

A curious thing. I was sitting on a rock under the phare a few sunsets ago when a child, a barefoot girl of about four clambered up the slope and insisted on filling my pockets with tiny shells from her apron. I told her in Flemish (I have now taken 43 lessons in it!) that I did not want them but she went on all the same. It was only after I had given her a coin and she had gone that I remembered the lighthouse of Patrick's papa in Boulogne and Caligula's order to his soldiers at the tower to gather up the seashells.

With kindest regards from all here to Miss Monnier and yourself

> *sincerely yours*
> *James Joyce*

P.S.

As I am writing I have just received complete G. Translation 900 typed pp. What shall I do with it? Goyert through Goll wired me that he wishes to come to see me.

> *Kindest regards*
> *J.J.*[35]

Joyce asks Beach to wait for a response from *The Dial* concerning the publication of the extract from *Work in Progress*.[36] He also explains that he will extend his stay by one or two days. Ultimately, the Joyce family remained in Ostend until 13 September. *Leopoldland* is an obvious reference to Leopold I and Leopold II, the first kings of Belgium (Albert I, the nephew of Leopold II, was on the throne in 1926). Joyce also cites 'La Revue', a reference to *La Revue nouvelle* (1924-1931), a Parisian monthly literary journal, published out of 2 rue Dufrénoy. The director was Y. Manuel-Lélis, whom Joyce had also met (by chance?) in Ostend. The city was undoubtedly a place of many unexpected and surprising encounters. *La Revue nouvelle* was internationally oriented and published contributions by Klaus Mann (1906-1949), Miguel de Unamuno (1864-1936), Franz Hellens (1881-1972), Edmond Jaloux (1878-1949), D. H. Lawrence (1885-1930), Henri Michaux (1899-1984) and Ivan Goll (1891-1950), amongst others. Between 1926 and 1928, it produced *Cendres* (in a translation by Yva Fernandez) and *Chamber music* (in a translation by Georges Duplaix).[37] Joyce also mentions having taken forty-three Flemish lessons (i.e. Dutch). It is interesting to speculate from whom

Joyce received this tuition. The schools would have been closed during the summer months. Was he able to secure the services of a private teacher? Could it have been Patrick Hoey who, having learnt some Dutch during his stay in Belgium, offered to teach his friend the rudiments of the language?

Joyce also mentions Georg Goyert (1884-1966), who translated *Ulysses* into German for the Rhein-Verlag publishing house in Basel, and the Franco-German poet Ivan Goll (1891-1950). In a fascinating passage at the end of his letter, Joyce describes an encounter with a little girl. He recalls that, while sitting on a rock in the vicinity of Ostend's lighthouse, he suddenly remembers Saint Patrick's father and the lighthouse in Boulogne. Saint Patrick (c. 385-461), whose original name is thought to have been Maewyn Succat, was the son of a Roman decurion named Calpurnius who governed a colony in England. His mother was Conchessa, who was related to Saint Martin of Tours. Calpurnius is also said to have been a guardian of the famous tower, or 'lighthouse', that was built by the Emperor Caligula on the cliffs near the city that we know today as Boulogne. According to William C. Fleming's book *Boulogne-sur-Mer: St Patrick's Native Town* (1907), Saint Patrick narrates in his autobiographical *Confessions* that he was born on the outskirts of a town called Bonaven, where there was a Roman encampment, and that as a young boy in his fifteenth year, he was taken prisoner by the Irish Scots. This event corresponds with a raid conducted by the Irish warlord, Niall of the Nine Hostages, into Armorica (Armoric Gaul or Brittany). As the Irish Scots invaded in the year that Saint Patrick turned fifteen, and since he identified his captors as belonging to the nation that he had converted, it is highly likely that he was taken prisoner during the aforementioned attack. As Bononia, or Boulogne-sur-Mer, was called Bonauen by the Gaulish Celts, and as the 'v' and 'u' are interchangeable in Gaelic, it might well be the same place that Saint Patrick describes as Bonaven in his *Confessions*. The Irish poet and writer Saint Fiacc (c. 415-520) declares that the Apostle of Ireland was born at Nemthur, the name given by the Gaulish Celts to Caligula's lighthouse on the outskirts of Bononia (modern-day Boulogne). The Roman tower was about 40-metres high and was restored in the 9th century by Charlemagne before it finally collapsed on 29 July 1644. It was also known as Tour d'Ordre or Tour d'Orde.

Joyce's encounter with the young girl seems to have been a kind of 'epiphany', one that is reminiscent of Saint Augustine's chance meeting with a child on a beach. Saint Augustine (c. 354-430) is known for his treatise *De Trinitate (About the Holy Trinity)*, the result of a thirty-year period of meditation upon the mystery of the Trinity. One day, as Augustine was walking along the seashore, pondering this enigma, he saw a small boy running back and forth between the waves and a small hole that he had dug in the sand. The boy was using a seashell to carry the water. Augustine approached and asked him, 'My boy, what are doing?' To which the child smiled sweetly and replied, 'I am trying to pour all of the sea into this hole.' 'But that is impossible, my dear child, the hole cannot contain so much water' said Augustine. The boy paused for a moment, stood up, looked into the eyes of the saint, and replied, 'It is no more impossible than what you are trying to do – comprehend the immensity of the mystery of the Holy Trinity with your small intelligence.' Reflecting upon the child's response, Augustine momentarily turned away. When he glanced down to ask him something else, he had vanished.[38]

According to Richard Ellmann, James Lyons, a relative of Joyce on his mother's side, flew from England to Ostend on 26 August 1926, spent a few hours with Joyce and immediately flew back home.[39]

On 26 August, Joyce sent a telegram from Ostend to Adrienne Monnier:

OSTENDE

TRADUCTION ALLEMANDE ULISSE [sic] *FINIE RECUE HIER SALUTATIONS CORDIALES = JAMES JOYCE*

26/8/1926

[Addressed to:
Adrienne Monnier chez
Josephine Gay Les Deserts [sic]
Savoie France][40]

Adrienne Monnier (1892-1955), a French bookseller, writer and publisher, was an influential figure in Parisian literary circles during the

1920s and 1930s. Monnier had opened a bookshop and lending library, *La Maison des Amis des Livres*, at 7 rue de l'Odéon on 15 November 1915. She was among the first Frenchwomen to own such an establishment. Having worked as a teacher and literary secretary, Monnier adored the writers and was determined to forge a career as a bookseller. With meagre resources, she opened her shop at a time of genuine need: a huge number of male booksellers had been forced to close their businesses when enlisted during the First World War. Monnier also offered advice and encouragement to Sylvia Beach, who would become a lifelong friend. In the 1920s the two women ran their shops opposite one another on the rue de l'Odéon in the heart of the Latin Quarter. Both establishments became meeting places for the French, British, and American writers in the city. In June 1925, Monnier, with Beach's encouragement and literary support, launched a French language review, *Le Navire d'Argent*. The French writer Jean Prévost (1901-1944) was installed as literary editor. Despite making a loss, it was an important part of the literary scene of the 1920s and helped to launch several writers' careers. Running to a hundred pages per issue, it was 'French in language, but international in spirit', and drew heavily upon the circle of writers frequenting Monnier's shop. The first edition contained a French translation (prepared jointly by Monnier and Beach) of T. S. Eliot's poem, *The Love Song of J. Alfred Prufrock* (May 1925). Other issues included an early draft excerpt from James Joyce's *Work in Progress* (October 1925). The March 1926 edition was devoted to American writers, including Walt Whitman (1819-1892), William Carlos Williams (1883-1963) and E. E. Cummings (1894-1962). Monnier, who was the first to introduce the work of Ernest Hemingway to French audiences by publishing his work in translation, also contributed work under the pseudonym of J.-M. Sollier, based on her mother's maiden name. After twelve issues, she abandoned *Le Navire d'Argent*, as it was too time-consuming and expensive to produce. To cover her losses, Monnier was forced to auction her collection of some 400 books, many of which contained personal dedications. A decade later, Monnier launched another periodical, the *Gazette des Amis des Livres*, which ran from January 1938 until May 1940.[41] In his telegram, Joyce informs her that he has received Georg Goyert's German translation of *Ulysses*, which was due to be published by Rhein-Verlag in Basel.

On 29 August (postmarked 30 August) Joyce wrote to Harriet Shaw Weaver:

Hôtel de l'Océan, Digue de Mer, Ostende

Dear Miss Weaver: These rapid lines are to wish you many happy returns of your birthday. I hope they reach you in time as I have found the post here rather slow – 2 days from Paris, a 5 hours run. I am sorry to hear your sister had such a time in the storm – a dreadful experience for an immobilised person! The only good thing is that sometimes a shock like that goes good and in any case a visitation of that kind rarely recurs…

I am of a sudden overladen with work. Last week the entire typescript of Ulysses *in German arrived and on top of it the German translator to revise it with me. We work together all day practically, word for word. They want to bring it out in October!!!*

I am sorry to hear Miss Marsden's trouble and of course do not bother about the disk in such circumstances. All the same I was glad to have your notes on my voice and would like more about my non-rhetorical accents when you feel so inclined.

I hope the German publisher won't rush the translation – and me.
With the renewed good wishes and kindest regards sincerely yours,

James Joyce [42]

That same day, he wrote a postcard to Sylvia Beach:

[Picture Postcard]
29 August 1926   *Hôtel Océan, Ostende*

Dear Miss Beach: I hope this finds you safe back in Paris after a pleasant holiday. Goyert arrived with the complete Ulysses *– to appear in October! They give only 14 days for revisions but it will take at least 6 weeks. Working morning an*[d] *afternoon in this heat. Thank Miss Monnier for copy of letter. And the* Dial*?*

With kindest regards
sincerely yours
James Joyce[43]

Georg Goyert probably arrived in Ostend on 28 August. Joyce asks Beach if there is news from *The Dial* regarding *Work in Progress*. It was not Book I, chapter 8, that had been accepted for publication by *The Dial*, prior to its volte-face, but an early version of Book III, the 'Four Watches of Shaun'.[44]

On 31 August (postal stamp), James Joyce sends a postcard to the French writer Valery Larbaud (1881-1947) who was then living at 71 bis, rue Cardinal Lemoine, Paris:

> *Hôtel Océan*
> *Ostende*
>
> *Nous venons de travailler ensemble sur la traduction allemande d'*Ulysse *et dînons ensemble.*
> *Salutations cordiales*
>
> > > *James Joyce*

Respects Joyce L. [written by Lucia Joyce][45]

Although Joyce was residing at the Hôtel de l'Océan, the postcard carries a picture of the Hôtel Helvetia, 62, Digue de Mer, Ostend. This may well have been establishment in which he dined with Georg Goyert. Joyce and Larbaud had been friends since late 1920, after meeting in Paris. In June 1921, the Joyce family had lived rent-free in Larbaud's apartment at 71 rue du Cardinal Lemoine. A letter survives from Larbaud to Sylvia Beach, dated February 1921, in which he conveys his admiration for *Ulysses*.[46]

On 31 August 1926, *L'Écho d'Ostende* publicised the operetta *Pas sur la bouche* (*Not on the Mouth*), which was scheduled to run at the Théâtre de la Scala in Ostend from 1-7 September. The music was by Maurice Yvain (1891-1965) and the libretto by André Barde (1874-1945). This did not escape Joyce's notice, since he cites the very same operetta in one of his famous Notebooks (VI.B.12).[47]

On 1 September 1926, Joyce wrote a letter in Italian to his son Giorgio in Paris:

Caro Giorgio: Se hai dato la tua demissione [dimissione] con quanti giorni di congedo puoi cavarsela e venire qui? Non ti daranno un aumento o se ne danno sarà minimo. Il mio cheque non è venuto oggi ma la sig. M. ti anticiperà tutto quanto ti occorre. Secondo me hai gran bisogno di cambiamento totale di vita. Dunque viene qui non necessariamente per restare ma almeno per un po' di giorni eppoi si vedrà.
Non mi sorprende che ti abbiano rifiutato una vacanza. Quello si chiama essere uomo d'affari, uomo pratico, giusto ecc. Dovresti pensare molto più alla tua fisica ed allo sfruttamento del dono naturale della voce che hai ed avrai.
Ti propongo allora di chiudere la casa ecc. e di telegrafarmi il giorno e la ora del tuo arrivo se questo piano ti va.

Puoi magari scaricare il biasimo sulle mie spalle dicendo al sig. Heischl che tuo padre non vuole che resti alla tua età tutto l'estate in un'atmosfera come quello di Parigi senza respirare un po' d'aria buona.

Non dimenticare la ricetta e sarei arcicontento di avere una fiala di gocce gialle' anche dalla sig.ra Allère.
I miei saluti al dott. B.
Ti abbraccio

Babbo

1/ix/926.[48]

In this paternal missive, Joyce not only encourages his son to make radical changes to his life but also to travel to Ostend, where he can enjoy the fresh air. He tells him to send a telegram with the date and the hour of his arrival. Although we do not know exactly when Giorgio arrived in Ostend, it could not have been prior to 4 September. Joyce refers to a Mr Heischl and a Mrs Allère, whose identities remain known. The former may have been one of his Giorgio's superiors at the bank where he was employed, while the latter might have been a neighbour or a friend.

31

On 1 September, Joyce sent a telegram from Ostend to Harriet Shaw Weaver, care of Dora Marsden, Glencoin, Glenridding, Penrith:

Many happy returns James Joyce [49]

The next day, he sent a letter to Sylvia Beach:

2 September 1926   *Hôtel de l'Océan, Ostende*

Dear Miss Beach: I am glad you are back safe and sound. Thanks for the mandat. All is well now financially.

   Did you get the extra corrections for Λabcd? If so, please add p. 111.1 22 for 'mayo' read 'mayom'. Also did you get the snapshots Lucia sent? Please say and if not I shall have new copies made.

   I return the clippings with this.

   I went word for word through the German translation for the 1ˢᵗ 100 pp. It is all right now. But it was a hard work especially as I did not know Mr Goyert or he me. He is all right but the Rheinverlag want to rush the publication for November at latest! And rush him. And me.

   Will you please send him to his address (George [sic] *Goyert, Ledderken, 13, Witten, Ruhr, Germany).*

   1) A copy of Gorman's book

   2) Gens de Dublin

   3) An accurate copy of the plan.

   4) 2 copies (if you can spare them) of the prospectus of 1st edition of U.

   He tells me there have been scores of articles about me in the German daily weekly and monthly press. Some of them 40 pages long! He will send you some of the dates.

   Has Clodd's Story of the Alphabet *come. A book I would like is:* La Jeunesse de Swift *by Emile Pons, editeur* [sic]*?*

   Goyert has left for Germany [.] *He returns to visit me in a few weeks and will stay a whole fortnight. As they announce the translation completely 'revised by the author' they must allow me time or I shall be obliged to publish a disclaimer. I told him so and he agreed with me.*

   The firm (R.V) has a wrong idea about the book, I think. But it can be set right.

                               With kindest regards

                               Sincerely yours

                               James Joyce

P.S. I am writing this in an awkward pose on a book balanced on my knee on Lucia's paper. Hence those scrawls. [50]

Joyce asks Sylvia Beach to prepare a copy of his instructions and send them to *The Dial*. The manuscript in the James Joyce Collection of the State University of New York (Buffalo) is an extra draft sheet that contains instructions to Beach to amend a missing copy of the second typescript of Book III of *Work in Progress*.[51] Joyce also enquires if she has received the photographs that Lucia has posted from Ostend (now part of the James Joyce Collection, State University of New York, Buffalo). Thanks to Joyce's letter, it is possible to establish relatively accurate dates for the photographs. Since the letter is dated 2 September, and James, Nora and Lucia Joyce arrived in Ostend on 5 or 6 August, the pictures must have been taken between 6 and 31 August. Allowing for the time needed to develop the prints from the negatives, we can narrow the time period yet further and suggest between 6 and 26 August. Since Patrick Hoey also appears in a number of photographs, we can deduce that Joyce met him on at least two occasions: in the *Pharmacie anglaise* and at some point around 15 August 1926. In all probability, the photographs were taken between 10 and 26 August. The images showing Giorgio Joyce could only have been taken after 1 September (the date of Joyce's letter inviting him to Ostend) and before 16 September 1926, the day upon which the Joyce family departed for Ghent. The fact that Lucia personally posted the prints to Sylvia Beach implies that she was the main photographer, although the pictures in which she herself features were most probably taken by Nora.

In the same letter, Joyce asks Sylvia Beach to send a number of items to Georg Goyert:

1. A copy of Gorman's book: a reference to *James Joyce: His First Forty Years* by Herbert Gorman (published by B.W. Huebsch, New York, 1924).
2. *Gens de Dublin*: the French translation of *The Dubliners*, published by Plon-Nourrit & Co., Paris, 1926.
3. The plan: a reference to *Ulysses* and the notes that Joyce had compiled around 1919-1920 as a way of helping his friend, the translator and writer Stuart Gilbert (1883-1969), understand the fundamental structure of the book. Gilbert published this plan in 1930 in his book, *James Joyce's* Ulysses: *A Study*. The first person to whom Joyce revealed the plan seems to have been the Italian writer and translator Carlo Linati (1878-1949).
4. Two copies of the prospectus of 1st edition of U: a reference to prospectus for *Ulysses* that was published in 1922 by Shakespeare & Co., Paris.

Joyce also mentions *The Story of the Alphabet* (1900) by the British anthropologist Edward Clodd (1840-1930), published in London by George Newnes Ltd., and *Swift, les années de jeunesse et le 'Conte du Tonneau'* (1925) by Émile Pons (1885-1964), published in Strasbourg by Librairie Istria. Émile Pons, a specialist on the work of Jonathan Swift, was Professor of Literature at the University of Strasbourg and later at the Sorbonne, Paris.

In his letter dated 5 November 1926 to his brother Stanislaus, Joyce recounts the arduous work that went into the German translation of *Ulysses*:

2 Square Robiac, 192 rue de Grenelle, Paris

Dear Stannie: I enclose Lire 6000. – in draft on Trieste and Milan. I hope it reaches you in time with our best wishes to Nelly and yourself. Let me know if you get it. I am utterly overworking myself. Roth is pirating Ulysses *(bowdlerized) in a new magazine of which he sells 50,000 copies a month. I have tried to enjoin the publication but there seems to be no remedy. The Germans, having given me four days at Ostende, to revise the translation with the translator (we did 88 pages) are now rushing the translation into print. It is of course full of the absurdest errors and with large gaps. Such is financial literature. If they do not give me a délai* [delay], *I shall ask Miss Beach to circularize the German press with a disclaimer.*
I hope your arrangements are all made and that your marriage will soon come off and that it will be a very happy one.

Buona fortuna!
Jim[52]

On 11 September, Joyce wrote to Sylvia Beach on stationary from Hôtel de l'Océan:

11 September 1926   Hôtel de l'Océan, Digue de Mer, Ostende

Dear Miss Beach: Many thanks for the telegram and good news. I have been over Λabcd all day and send you these final corrections. Please copy and send on. Miss Moore may consult Who's Who *or Biographical Notes to Gorman's book.*
Λabcd is a title sign or private mark for myself like the others, for reference.

She may use some such title as Ford or Walsh or The Criterion *used. If she likes I will read the proof. When does it start to come out?*

In great haste
with kindest regards
sincerely yours
James Joyce

P S. Yes I got your letter – delayed – from Les Deserts [sic].[53]

Joyce, who was still occupied with *Work in Progress*, is thus sending the final version of Λabcd, or in other words the 'Four Watches of Shaun'.[54] He also refers to the American poet and critic Marianne Moore (1887-1972), then editor of *The Dial* (a post she held from 1925 to 1929). It was Moore who had initially accepted the excerpt of Joyce's *Work in Progress* for publication before dramatically changing her mind. Moore's first professionally published poems had appeared in the American magazine *The Egoist*, a feminist publication that had been founded by Dora Marsden (1882-1960) but converted into a literary review by Ezra Pound. 'Gorman's book' is a reference to the biography, *James Joyce. His First Forty Years*, which had been published by Huebsch (New York) in 1924. The English writer Ford Madox Ford (1873-1939) and the American poet Ernest Walsh (1895-1926) are also cited in the letter. In 1924, Ford Madox Ford had published the first part of Joyce's new work in a special *Work in Progress* supplement to the *Transatlantic Review*. The title *Work in Progress* was not amended until Joyce finally published his novel as *Finnegans Wake* in 1939. This was not because he did not have a title in mind, but because he did not want to divulge it prior to publication. Joyce believed that the title of a book should not precede the work itself, and that, moreover, his readers ought not to be able to guess the title from the extracts that had been published during its long genesis (a total of seventeen years).[56] 'Walsh' is a reference to Ernest Walsh, a young American poet who had arrived in Paris in 1922 and become part of the avant-garde literary scene on the Left Bank. His was in frail health, suffering from both tuberculosis and the injuries that he had sustained in a plane crash while training to be a pilot during First World War. After running out of money, Walsh ended up ill and penniless in one of the city's grandest hotels. He was rescued by Ezra Pound, who settled his debts and took him under his wing. Walsh went on to marry the British poet and suffragette Ethel Moorhead (1869-1955), who became his patron and collaborator on the literary journal *This Quarter*. He was later assisted by the American novelist Kay Boyle (1902-1992), whom he subsequently married. Walsh and Boyle moved the offices of their journal to Grasse, on the French Riviera, where the climate was easier for Walsh to tolerate. *This Quarter* featured new writing by, amongst others, both Pound and Joyce. The second issue (Autumn-Winter 1925) published the 'Shem the Penman' section from Joyce's *Work in Progress* along with two photographs of Joyce. It also included an extract of the unfinished opera, *Mr Bloom and the Cyclops*, by the American composer George Antheil (1900-1959), which was inspired by the 'Cyclops' episode of *Ulysses*. Walsh died of tuberculosis in October 1926.[57] Joyce also mentions the English quarterly review *The Criterion*, founded in 1922, which was known as *The New Criterion* between 1926 and 1927. The first issue, dated October 1922, included T. S. Eliot's *The Waste Land* and a lecture by Valery Larbaud on *Ulysses*. *The Criterion* also published an extract of Joyce's *Work in Progress*. T. S. Eliot was the long-time editor of this prestigious review.

On 13 September, Joyce sent a telegram to Sylvia Beach, in which he announces his departure for Ghent:

[TELEGRAM]

OSTENDE

= *HOTEL POSTE GHENT KINDEST REGARDS* = *JAMES JOYCE* +

13/9/1926[58]

From a letter dated 26 February 1927, which Joyce sent to his old friend Claud W. Sykes (1883-1964), we also know that the author met a Dutchman called Juda de Vries (alias Jules Martin) while holidaying in Ostend. Joyce had met him before, in Zurich, during the First World War:

2 Square Robiac 192 rue de Grenelle, Paris

Dear Mr Sykes: Yes. Ulysses has been done by the same man. It is not his fault, he is forced to do it on time. The edition will be dear (£10 a copy) very luxurious etc and not scamped. I cannot control them completely but something I can do. Proofs will be sent to you 100 pp at a time. It is very kind of you to say you will look through them. Any ideas that occur you may jot down in the margin. Thanks very much.

I got your novel from your publishers. I think I shall start to find out the mystery as soon as this lawsuit is well launched. I hope it sells well. I will send you the opening pages of my new book, a piece which will appear here 15 March. If you can solve its ninetynineangular mystery will you please let me know…

We are glad to learn Mrs Sykes and yourself are well. At Ostende this summer we met Devries [de Vries] *who is there pulling all the teeth and legs he can.*[59]

In the spring of 1917, while Joyce and de Vries were both in Zurich, the latter had tried to persuade Joyce to write a film scenario.[60] Richard Ellmann writes:

> During this spring of 1917 Joyce received a visit from a small, dark-haired young man named Jules Martin, as he called himself. Though insignificant in appearance, Martin has grandiose ideas. He was trying to set up a music hall in the Holbeinstrasse, and was also full of a plan to move into film making, which had advanced as far as some stationery headed 'New York Film Studio'. Joyce, immediately ready to garner some of the film profits which the Volta in Dublin had failed to yield, listened with interest to Martin's proposals. Martin had a scenario with the not unpredictable title of *Wine, Women, and Song*; Joyce had only to retouch it here and there, and then Martin would secure a cast.[61]

At the time, Joyce was struggling to support his family and working as an English teacher and voice coach. Viewing de Vries' project as a solution to his financial difficulties, he accepted the job. Claud W. Sykes, a former actor who had previously worked with English impresario Sir Herbert Beerbohm Tree (1852-1917), was to be his assistant. This speculative venture soon collapsed, but Sykes suggested the establishment of a resident company to present English plays in Zurich. Sykes would be the producer and director while Joyce could run the business. To this end, they established a company called 'The English Players'. A handwritten receipt from Juda de Vries appears in Joyce's Zurich Notebook.[62] Before the year was out, however, de Vries was arrested for embezzlement. According to Bruce Stewart, he was the son of a distinguished Dutch gynaecologist who wrote to Joyce to thank him for his kindness when the 'miscreant' was imprisoned in Lausanne.[63] A description of Juda de Vries can also be found in *James Joyce and the making of 'Ulysses'*, which was published in 1934 by Grayson & Grayson in New York. The book was written by the British painter Frank Budgen (1882-1971), who was one of Joyce's friends. Budgen writes:

> Robed in fine linen, with canary gloves and patent leather shoes, another Dutchman walks the town, sometimes in company of James Joyce. He is dentist, cinema producer, dealer in shirtwaists, synthetic pearls and synthetic bouillon. His is Juda Devries *[sic]*, alias Joe Martin, alias Jules Moreau. He has written a film scenario entitled *Wine, Woman and Song,* and he writes letters on pink notepaper headed with the crossed flags of the allied nations. His father is the venerable gynaecologist of Amsterdam. Joyce was once instrumental in getting him out of jail into hospital, and he, being as ingenious as he was enterprising, made a wooden money-box in the form of a Bible for his serviable [sic] friend. It bore, by way of title, 'My First Success', by James Joyce.[64]

Many years later, Joyce would mention Juda de Vries (spelled *Devries*) again, this time on a postcard written from Lausanne, dated 23 August 1938, addressed to his biographer Herbert Gorman (1893-1954):

> *I saw Giorgio* [Joyce's son] *yesterday. He thinks that Devries's real name should not be mentioned (an initial not D or any other name instead) as he belongs to a very well known Amsterdam family and has also, it seems, 'made good' at last. I don't know how it escaped me.*
>
> *J.J.*[65]

A note by Stuart Gilbert also refers to Juda de Vries:

> In Gorman's *James Joyce*, p. 243, Juda de Vries appears under the name of 'Joe Martin'. De Vries was an errant acquaintance of Joyce in Zurich; he later became a respected dentist in Brussels. His letters to Joyce are at Cornell.[66]

Joyce is apparently asking Herbert Gorman to omit Juda de Vries' name from his biography, which was eventually published by Rinehart & Company (New York) in 1948. Gorman had published an earlier biography of Joyce, entitled *James Joyce: His First Forty Years*, in 1924 (B. W. Huebsch, New York). Gorman did not, however, follow Joyce's instructions to the letter. In his monograph on Joyce, he writes:

There were humorous characters to be encountered too, the flotsam and jetsam of half a dozen countries, and one at least among them had a brief indirect influence on Joyce's career. Joyce knew him first under the name of Joe Martin. It was not his real name but for various reasons that must be suppressed. Joe Martin, then, waited upon the Irish writer one day in the spring of 1917 and made the astonishing proposal that Joyce write a cinema scenario for him, its title to be *Wine, Women and Songs*. 'We'll get wealthy women into it,' explained Martin, 'women in fur pelts. We'll teach them how to walk and then charge them a fee for being in the film.' Later Joyce discovered that the astute Mr. Martin proposed to shoot his picture without any film at all in the camera; in other words, the project was a barefaced swindle to be based on the vanity of the 'women in fur pelts.' […] Some time later (still in springtime) Joe Martin sent to Joyce as an assistant in the preparation of the scenario Mr. Claud W. Sykes, an actor who had played in the company of Sir Herbert Beerbohm Tree. It was because he was the connecting link, so to speak, between Joyce and Mr. Sykes that Joe Martin was of indirect influence on the Irish writer's career in Zurich. […] For instance, Joyce was instrumental in getting Joe out of prison and into hospital at one time. […] It was at this time that Joyce discovered, by receiving a letter of profuse gratitude from Joe's aged father in Amsterdam and thanking him for the efforts on behalf of the 'black sheep of my family,' that Joe was in reality the son of a well-known gynaecologist in a large European city. From prison Joe-Jules-Judas was transferred to the hospital. 'This time I am all in,' he wrote to Joyce. But he wasn't. For a brief period he acted as prompter for the English players. Then he disappeared. Six years or so later Joyce ran across him in Ostend. He was in good health, well-dressed and the owner of a large motorcar and a house in Brussels. And from there he disappears of Joyce's life. Rumour, however, has it that he has reformed and is now a pillar of respectability.[67]

Juda de Vries eventually became a respectable dentist in Brussels, 'pulling all the teeth and legs he can' (as Joyce wrote to Sykes). A dentist named 'U. de Vries', domiciled at 2, rue d'Accolay, Brussels, is listed in the 1926 edition of the *Almanach du Commerce et de l'Industrie*. It is not known if this is the same Juda de Vries.

Joyce, who was a good Latinist, must have realised that the name 'Ostend' means different things in different languages. The Dutch name for the city, 'Oostende', translates as 'at the east end': a reference to the city's medieval location on the eastern tip of the peninsula known as *Testerep* (or *Ter Streep*), now subsumed by the sea. The French spelling for the city is 'Ostende'. In Latin, however, *ostende* is the present singular imperative of the verb *ostendere*, which means 'to show'. It is perhaps worth noting that Joyce used the form *ostenditur* (third singular passive indicative of *ostendere*) in *Finnegans Wake*:

> (for – husk, hisk, a spirit spires – Dolph, dean of idlers, meager suckling of gert stoan, though barekely a balbose boy, he too, – *venite, preteriti, sine mora dumque de entibus nascituris decentius in lingua romana mortuorum parva chartula liviana* **ostenditur**, *sedentes in letitiae super ollas carnium, spectanted immo situm lutetiae unde auspiciis secundis tantae consurgent humanae stirpes, antiquissimam flaminum amborium Jordani et Jambaptistae mentibus revolvamus sapientiam: totum tute fluvii modo mundo fluere, eadem quae ex aggere fututa fuere iterum inter alveum fore futura, quodlibet sese ipsum per aliudpian agnoscere contrarium, omnem demun amnem ripis rivalibus amplecti* – recurrently often, when him moved he would cake their chair,...[68].

Joyce's use of the neologisms 'ostscent' and 'Ostenton' in *Finnegans Wake* are also a plausible references to the city of Ostend, and to the famous summer storm of 16 August 1926:

> - Did it now blow some gales, westnass or **ostscent**, rather strongly to less, allin humours out of turn, jusse as they rose and sprungen?[69]
> - ... ; who repulsed from his burst the bombolts of **Ostenton** and falchioned each flash downsaduck in the deep;....[70]

ANNEXES

I.

Regarding the manuscript of a chapter of *Finnegans Wake*
as catalogued in The James Joyce Collection, University at Buffalo, The
State University of New York:

*VI.I.42.a [See <u>X.C.107</u> (X.C.101)]: 'Work in Progress'/*Finnegans Wake*
Emendations and Errata: Emendations for a (Missing) Duplicate Copy of
the Second Typescript of Book III/*Finnegans Wake* III.1–4 (1926):
<u>Material Description and Collation</u>: The manuscript consists of 2 loose
sheets of Hôtel de l'Océan, Ostende, Belgium, stationery; the emendations
are in Joyce's hand in black ink and lead pencil and in Beach's hand in
black ink. It was enclosed with Joyce's letter to Beach dated 2 September
1926 but was only catalogued after the publication of *JJSB*.
<u>Measurements</u>: The sheets measure 21.3 x 27.5 cm.
<u>Contents</u>: The manuscript is an extra draft sheet that contains instructions
to Beach to emend a missing copy of the second typescript of Book III.
Joyce asked Beach to prepare a copy of these instructions and send them
to *The Dial* (see MS VI.I.40.b for a copy of one of three of the errata sheets
that were sent to the printer; Beach to Marianne Moore, 16 September
1926, in Keri Walsh's *The Letters of Sylvia Beach* [New York: Columbia
University Press], p. 112). See FW 403.23, 405.23–24, 406.02, 406.04–05,
406.17–18, 406.30, 407.29, 411.05, 419.24, 419.31, 422.17, 425.09–10, 429.18,
430.01, 430.02, 451.20–21, 456.27, 456.30, 456.35, 463.06, 463.07, 465.18,
478.26, 484.18, 495.12, 524.03, 532.10, 557.15, 558.20 562.03–04, 565.36,
570.33, 571.03, 577.17, 579.18 (or 579.22), 580.09, 584.05, and 589.07.
<u>JJA Draft Code</u>: III§<u>1A.7+/1D.7+//2A.7+/2B.5+/2C.7+//3A.6+/3B.6+//4.3+</u>.
<u>Dating</u>: The manuscript was probably written on 11 September 1926.
<u>Publication</u>: This manuscript is unpublished but Joyce's letter in which this
manuscript was enclosed was published in JJSB70–71 (#84).
<u>Other Markings</u>: Joyce headed the recto of the first sheet 'Λabcd' in the
upper left corner in black ink. Joyce presumably added the emendation
in lead pencil in the lower margin on the first sheet after he written the
others. After this, Beach added yet another emendation in black ink, based
on the instructions from Joyce in MS X.C.106 (X.C.100). It was probably
Beach who wrote the question mark beside an emendation on the first
sheet in black ink.

II.
Regarding another person named Patrick Hoey of Dublin:

Another person named Patrick Hoey is mentioned in the register of the census organised on 31 March 1901. He was 29 years old in 1901, thus born in 1872, and domiciled at Mountjoy Street. He is mentioned as a librarian and married. On the other hand, he is not mentioned in the census of 1911. This Patrick J. Hoey, former library assistant at the Capel Street and Thomas Street branches, was the Chief Assistant at the Thomas Street Public Library and was appointed librarian in charge at the newly built Charleville Mall Public Library in 1899. In the following year he took on the supervision of Clontarf Public Library in addition to Charleville Mall. Under Hoey's management, Charleville Mall was particularly successful and resulted in plans for an extension in 1910 assisted by a grant provided through Andrew Carnegie, United Kingdom and Ireland Trust. Unfortunately, Patrick Hoey was dismissed in 1907 'in consequence of some irregularities in the administration of Charleville Mall and Clontarf Public Libraries'.[1] P. J. Hoey is mentioned in the *Freeman's Journal*, dated 24 June 1910, and cited in *The Irish Book in English 1891-2000* of *The Oxford History of the Irish Book*:

> 'The Lending Department has already proved successful beyond even the most sanguine expectations', P. J. Hoey, the librarian of the Charleville Mall Public Library on Dublin's North Strand declared after its opening in December 1900.[2]

[1] *Dublin City Public Libraries 1884-2009: 125 years of service to the community* taken from the transcript of a talk to commemorate 125 years of Public Library Service in Dublin City by Deirdre Ellis-King, Dublin City Librarian as part of Local History Day 26th September 2009.
[2] Clare Hutton (ed.), *The Oxford History of the Irish Book. Volume V: The Irish Book in English 1891-2000*, Oxford University Press, 2011, p. 57.

III.

Letters written by Juda (alias Jules) de Vries, dating from 1917, to James
Joyce in the James Joyce collection, #4609, box 7, Division of Rare and
Manuscript Collections, Cornell University Library, New York, Ithaca:

[written in black pencil]

[printed heading]

New-York-Film-
    Stüdio
~~Kreuzstrasse 38~~ [crossed]
Rehalp.[1] [added]   Telephon 107 22
                                                    ~~8911~~ [crossed]
                                                    170 [added]

My dear Mr. Joyes [sic].

*Sorry I was not able to see
you all this week but as I have
had bits of trouble, I also like to
give you my new address quite
close to you Flora strasse 48*[2] *Post
R by my self* [sic] *as I could not
stand it any longer at home
will explain all to you when
I see you again.*
            Yours very truly
                Jules

[printed at bottom of paper letter]

Manufactures of high class films and Motion pictures dramatic and comique.
JULES MARTIN . LATE STAR and DIRECTOR OF THE LEADING
AMERICAN FILMS CO,S.

[1] Rehalp is a small locality on the border between Zurich and the
municipality of Zollikon.
[2] In 1917, Joyce was domiciled in Zurich at the Seefeldstrasse, 54 and
Seefeldstrasse, 73. The Florastrasse crosses the Seelfeldstrasse.

[written in black pencil]

Saturday St Croix[1]
The 12ᵗʰ V. 17.   5.30 ᴾᴹ

My dear Mʳ Joyes [sic].

     Your P. C. of the 9ᵗʰ to hand, and | I was told already by the Judge | here that I can have a defenseur [défenseur = defence attorney] *| free from the state, But as | it is a complicate* [complicated] *case and | need a good preparation ahead | a time wich* [which] *will set me free | sooner in stead* [instead] *of writing so | long, and by paying a lawyer | his fair and small expenses | ahead to come and see me | so as he can prepaire* [prepare] *his [?]rief | and further I am sorry to say | but have not even one cent | to gett* [get] *a piece of bread with I | have had very little when I came | here – and with telephones Etc. || was it soon going – and now | I wrote to 54 but only a reply | came not to troble* [trouble] *here, after | I have been putting up for | here for one year that is | the thanks I have for it | not even one cent sinds* [since] *I | am here or some thing* [something] *propre* [propper] *to eat Can you | immagine* [imagine] *a hearth* [heart] *of a | woman like it, and is | all for <u>here</u> that I am | here I will explain it | all to you when I return | but I will do the same | on my return just wait. | the day she left here she told | the wife of the caporal to | take care of me for my | meals but she has not || left the cash for it this | [illegible word] I cannot expect | them to do this for nothing | you can just immagine* [imagine] *the | regular food that is giving* [given] *| at present, so bad and I | am not able touch it | nothing to eat nothing to | smoke o it terible* [terrible]*, but | why should I troble* [trouble] *you | with all this well I | tell you you have been | realy* [really] *the only one that | has done some thing* [something] *| for me. you must not | think that I am doing | time well this is not | the case but I was | told that this trubinale* [tribunal, court] *| the main G[?] is at m. || service and there fore* [therefore] *I | must wait his return to | go to Grandson[2] wich* [which] *I | hope will be soon, I have | also send* [sent] *you my Pown* [pawn] *| tickets to please help me | out with a little money if | you are in a position to | do so, you could keep them | as security, but if it is | imposible* [impossible] *for you self may | be you would be able to | give them to some one els* [else] *| to hold, but for all you do | dont* [don't] *lett* [let] *them come in the | hand of this swindelers* [swindlers] *| at 54[3], the* [they] *have done suficient* [sufficient] *| for the present to me to last me | for the rest of my day's, I am so | glad that my Landlord has kept | my things, as the Brother has || been trying to obtain them | but thank God no luck | for him; I expect several | lettres* [letters] *there would you | please see now and then | when you [illegible word] – how do | you like the singsires* [?] *| I have send* [sent] *you but I | see by the copie* [copy] *I have | forgotten where she gives | birth to the son he is | afterwards taken and placed | in a* [an] *incubator very | interesting point for the*

44

/ public I think to show / on the film, […] *please / write me By return what is /
done up till* [until] *now I am so //* interesting to hear about it / all, and by this
fine [?] */ wheather* [weather] *to pass valuable / time like this it is just / a shame.*
well to morrow [tomorrow] */ is again sunday and will /* [illegible word] *for
better I can / only say the fool I was / to take the blame for a / women* [woman]
en [and?] *me, and to / receive this in return / well must close please / write soon
with / fonderst* [fondest?] [illegible word] *to all*

Jules

[1] Sainte-Croix is a municipality of the canton of Vaud, Switzerland.
[2] Grandson is a municipality in the canton of Vaud, Switzerland.
[3] Seefeldstrasse 54 in Zurich where Joyce was domiciled in 1917.

[written in black ink]
[heading: Pénitencier (= Prison) Lausanne]

the 14th1917.

Dear Mr Joyes [sic],

    I thank you again for P.C. [postcard] *to haved / hear That my Father send me a com- / plained* [complaint] *that I have not send* [sent] *a card or / letter to my mothers unnivesairre* [anniversary] *but I surposes* [presume] *you have mixed them / up by sending as this was the card / to be send* [sent] *on the 24ᵗʰ of last month / to be at home for the 30ᵗʰ of Juin* [June] */ My father also writes to me that my / brother Jacque* [sic] *has met with a very / serious accedent* [accident] *and this is the reason / he has not answerd* [answered] *my last letter / I am sending enclose a P.C.* [postcard] *wich / you would kindly post for me. but / kindly see first if there is no stamp / of anny* [any] *kint* [kind] *on it if so take / it off. I only have a 5c.* [centimes] *one I am / sorry to say so will you please put / a 5C* [centimes] *to it I am sorry to give you / all this troble* [trouble], *but I wich* [wish] *I could do otherwise I am sure as time / seems very long I can asure* [assure] *you / and I am so unhappy. but what / can I do, I only can have patience / a note which I have recieved* [received] *from my Lady in / the Flora strasse but she must be patient / till I return, or when my Brother is up again / I trust he will send me some, and I will / pay up all. I will not run away with the 17p. / lines what is the reason are you mad at me / if so please tell me the reason will you please / or are you still ill I hope not. Well will close for / this time and remain your very sincerrely* [sincerely].

                                Jules

[verso, written vertically]

My father say's [says] *if he receive some writing or new again / From me than he will at once tell me all about / the accident that my Brother had wich* [which] *he say's* [says] */ see to be very very serious. Has Mr Legy told anny* [any] */thing of this at all? –*

[written in black ink]

Grandson the 31th 1917.
Chez monsieur Le Sergent
de la Gendarmerie

My dear Mr Joyes [sic],

   I surpose [presume] *you have been surprised that | I have not yett* [yet] *thanked you for the | correspondences you have forwarde* [forward] *to me | several day's ago, and I was looking | for a word from you also, the only | reason I could think of was that you | have still been ill, I realy* [really] *do hope | it is all better at present, which have | been the case with my self I have had | the Doctor to call on me sometimes | twice day'ly* [daily]*, well it is at present 6 | weeks that I am waiting, one is bound | to get ill, but I thank the lord | that I am better again must still | keep up taken the medicine.*

   I have spoken to my defenseur [defender: lawyer] *| and he will see what he can do, but for nothing, I don't show well it | cant be helped he also told me | why did I take all responsibility's on me. for this women he told me he has take up here Refferences* [references] *which where very bad indeed wich may help. You see she is suise* [swiss] *and I am a stranger | here, I have asked you in my last if this | avocate* [lawyer] *you have spoken to for me is your | own or the one of Mrs Burg becose* [because] *I | better prepare things ahead a time as | I do not know wich* [which] *may turn up | I also hope you do not mind and | that you think I am abusing of good | nature to ask you to have my corespon- | dence come to your address* [address] *but I | trust you where I have no one els* [else] *| to be friend of mine I soon to have | a day to be able to have a day to | show my apriciation* [appreciation] *for it. it is just hard luck and it cured* [cursed?] *me | for the rest of my day's* [days] *I can | assure you I am so glad that this | peoples are so good to me the best way | one can expect but anny* [any] *way to let me | write the way I want. also to give me my | letters unopened. well I will close for this | time and that you will give me a answer | By return of mail. How is the kind shule* [Schule: school] *school] going on.*

I oblige
with kind regards
from Jules

P.S.
Will you kindly mail thise [these] *letters*
I thanks [sic] *for same ----*

[written in black-purple pencil] [undated 1917]

Juge de Paix [Justice of the Peace]
St Croix[1]

My dear Mr Joyes [sic],

    As I am in great troble [trouble] / *principaly* [principally] *about here I must / try to secure a sertain* [certain] *amount / of money or security and as / I have the sympaty* [sympathy] *from the public / here, I was thinking the only / way would be to translate my <u>verfurering</u>* [?] *in to <u>Brochure</u> en / Français writ-ten ready so as I / can have same printed here for / Suise* [Suisse] *Française I hope I am not / asking you to* [too] *much all other / peoples have going against / me, but I hope you have / rewaind* [?] *my only friend I think / my life of late would make / you a book of value, my / hearth* [heart] *is broken from chame* [shame] / *but please forgive as a men* [man] / *of the world. Kindly answer / by return express if possible if you care I have / the permission of the juge - // While think Engagment* [?] *has come / from France. Will you please / send a Poste* [Post] *Card to say /*

Docteur Buckley Dentiste[2]
Rue des Paradis
Marseille
France

    Sorry but cannot come at / present will write to you / later, thanking you for / the past and hope to be / able to make use of your / offer soon……….. obliged.

Respectfully yours
J. de Vries
Zurich

[1] Sainte-Croix is a municipality of the canton of Vaud, Switzerland.
[2] Dr Buckley was an American dentist, domiciled at 81, rue Paradis, in Marseille. He stopped his practice after WW I.

[written in black ink] [undated 1917]

My dear Mr Joyes [sic],

    Thanks again for card to | hand, and I am glad to hear you are | a little better, so am I in health but not | in my situations, to morrow [tomorrow] *I am | to leave this place for Lausanne | as I do not nkow* [know] *yet what I am | up against there for I am sending you | some cards for my home in advance | which I should be very much obliged | if you would kindly send them | starting from the 24th of this month | say every 10 or 15 day's one. so as to | last, as I would not for the world my | old Parents to hear of it; so please | also keep this secret for my enemies in | Zurich as I nkow* [know] *you will; I did not | put anny* [any] *date as it dus* [does] *not | mather* [matter]; *the answers that come you | will kindly for the present till I | write to you, send them to the Préfet* [prefect] *du* [of] *| district a* [à: at] *Grandson.*[1] *– in case there are | anny* [any] *letters returned to you, please | dont return them again to Holland | just keep them till my return. again | now I expect some answers by now | from all this large Film firms in | Italy that I wrote before I left at the | Flora strasse 48. would you please when you | pass ask if there is anny* [any] *answer - | you dont* [don't] *need to send them on | to me you could open them | your self and if you think of | anny* [any] *importance you could answer | or do as you like with them | it may be very good for the future | well you will see – please also tell | the lady there if there should anny* [any] *one | come from 54*[2] *to clame* [claim] *some of | my things not to leave anny one | take anny thing I will pay here* [her] *| the amount my self on my | return, and clame* [claim] *my things personally | I have been done suficient harm at | present to lost me for the rest of | my day's by this peoples – now as to my Pown* [Pawn] *Tickets would you kindly | watch out if the time comes to write | to the loan House. at the adress* [address] *you | will see written on the heading of | the tickets to kindly keep them over | till my return and I will pay. the differences of intrest* [interest] *on same as | this is all I have left in this world | and would not like to loose it - | I hope you will pardon me. one's* [once] *| again to have put you to all this | troble* [trouble] *but when my time will | be up, it will be my plase* [pleasure] *to | show my selfe* [self].*

    I have had 5 minutes of | plasure [pleasure] *last sunday when I received your Poste Card hearing about | Bruckner now his turn comes | to have spoken bad behind my | back after I have been good to | him and not to stick to my | side, and also to hear that Mrs Burg is giving instruction | How can anny* [any] *person succeed in Buisseaus* [?] *in | this way. now will you believe | me. as to what I have always's | told you – well this will be the | end of the kino shule* [Kino Schule: Cinema School] *– in case you should see or speak | to her, try please do try to |*

keep things quite for me to be | able to regain and to explain | all not that I will be taken | again when I leave here by | here true here hostly [hostile?] *actions. | it was good that I have had | this letters from here where the | synario* [scenario] *she stated was my one | and this was a good proof | at all helpes* [helps] *– well I will close for this time, and I hope you | will understand my bad | scribbeling* [scribbling].
I dont know if it | is weakness or what it is | but I see dubbel [double] *– and have not had a drop for so | long now it must be very | hot in Zurich – I pitty you. | onless* [Unless] *you like the Hot wheather* [weather] *| will close for this time and | thanks for all + obliged*

From a very true friend
Jules

[1] Grandson is a municipality in the canton of Vaud, Switzerland.
[2] Seefeldstrasse, 54, in Zurich where Joyce was domiciled in 1917.

[written in purple pencil] [undated 1917]

*My dear M*ʳ *Joyes* [sic]. *Your letter and card to | hand   very manny* [many] *thanks for same | I cannot tell you how thankfull* [thankful] *I am | and how much I apriciate* [appreciate] *that dont* [don't] *| feel down on me, I hope I will soon | be able to explain to you why I am | kept here but thank God to day* [to-day] *I had | some good news and I hope I soon will | be able to go free again, I ask the Judge | about what you said for the connsulate* [consulate] *in | Neuchatel* [Neuchâtel] *but while the war is on it is | not excepted* [accepted?]*, but how ever I have material | for a* [an] *eccelente* [excellent] *comedy from the experi- ence | I have had here sinds* [since] *I am here I better | not write about it, but it is material | that will sell very good for your books | Just your style, please pardon this bad | writing by I must feel my way I am | so weak or my eyes are so bad I can | hardly see I do which I could have a | pair of my glasses that are in N° 48*[1] *| pardon me for the loan of the money to buy | a Lawyer and I will send you my pown* [pawn] *| tickets as security, for same, but it is || to be so stony broke as I am and that all | for the start of the assocation* [association]*, I only | which I could write and explain this | to M*ʳˢ *Burg I would do so in a minute | but there was no need of a reciced* [receipt] *| for manucript* [manuscript]*, but what pleased | the Judge here so that she has not | taken anny* [any] *proceeding against me | unfortuly* [unfortunately] *for me he say's* [says] *of this | mishap* [misstep?] *here, but you may tell here | I will show dubbel* [double] *my inergy* [energy] *on | my return we must arrange it so |that I spit and you have ones* [once] *started in it to remain with us | as you and here understand things | moor* [more] *in a comercial* [commercial] *way where I do in a practical point of veuw* [view] *| you will please look for a letter in the writing Desk at the Rehalp | of a Real Operator one that has | machien* [machine] *and understand the complete | action of fading in and out wich* [which] *| is requierd* [required] *for this film I also | would advice* [advise] *you to tell Mrs B | to give Mr Bruckner notice in time | She told me she as a* [an] *opperator* [operator] *from || arrow if I am not mistaken and on my | return I will teach him the same as | I have done Mr B what he knows at | present I have told you Right allong* [along] *| if from me, by the way while I am | here the Judge gave me the permission | to see and speak to whom I want | So spoke to a men* [man] *with great interprise* [en- terprise?] *| here and plenty of cash wich* [which] *seem | to like my idee* [idea]*, you can also tell | Mrs B that I am alone and by my | self and will remain alone to bring | this interprise* [enterprise] *wich* [which] *we have started | to a head and success but it takes | time the world was not made in one | day, see please if you could not| clear me while you are good with | here* [her] *to make here write a letter to me | as to here future continuation | without harming me wich* [which] *would only | harm here moor* [more] *than me I made a hard | start for here* [her] *but it is pas and I | know she and I we will be succesfull* [successful] *| here after. the working has not yett* [yet] *come | but will be here I think at 4 30*

train | thank you ever so much for it and | please note down all partners and expenses | you have for me will return same on my | return, I surpose [suppose] *you have to put your | dubbel* [double] *glasses on to read my scribeling* [scribbling] *but | I can hardly see my self* [myself]. *Have you | had anny* [any] *rehersals* [rehearsals] *yet* [yet] *and what have | you taken, I am very interesting to | hear, please pardon me if I am giving | you to* [too] *much troble* [trouble], *have the new people | materialize as Mrs B told me she had 50 6 contracts for this month. | how do you make for this people[s] in | the evening* [?] *only, dont* [don't] *forgett* [forget] *that | in the contract is arranged for the | Propriter* [proprietor?] *of the Rehalp[2] to put this | large* [illegible word] *up that he has that | will also make a good impression | Mr Ganti* [or Gonti?] *the men* [man] *who made the | decoration and tomb stone should | be p[…] as this is still of late | when we where in partnership will | you please see that this man gets his | money there is only a small Balance | Bruckner knows of it also well | I will close for this time and I hope | to hear from you soon as it cheers | me up as you are the only one where | I gett* [get] *corespondense* [correspondence] *from, again manny* [many] *| thanks, from you very truly friend.*
Jules

[1] In 1917, Jules de Vries was domiciled in Zurich at 48, Florastrasse.
[2] Rehalp is a small locality on the border between Zurich and the municipality of Zollikon.

IV. Herbert Gorman on 'Joe Martin' (Juda [Jules] de Vries):

There were humorous characters to be encountered too, the flotsam and jetsam of half a dozen countries, and one at least among them had a brief indirect influence on Joyce's career. Joyce knew him first under the name of Joe Martin. It was not his real name but for various reasons that must be suppressed. Joe Martin, then, waited upon the Irish writer one day in the spring of 1917 and made the astonishing proposal that Joyce write a cinema scenario for him, its title to be *Wine, Women and Songs*. 'We'll get wealthy women into it,' explained Martin, 'women in fur pelts. We'll teach them how to walk and then charge them a fee for being in the film.' Later Joyce discovered that the astute Mr. Martin proposed to shoot his picture without any film at all in the camera; in other words, the project was a barefaced swindle to be based on the vanity of the 'women in fur pelts.' […] Some time later (still in springtime) Joe Martin sent to Joyce as an assistant in the preparation of the scenario Mr. Claud W. Sykes, an actor who had played in the company of Sir Herbert Beerbohm Tree. It was because he was the connecting link, so to speak, between Joyce and Mr. Sykes that Joe Martin was of indirect influence on the Irish writer's career in Zurich. […] For instance, Joyce was instrumental in getting Joe out of prison and into hospital at one time. […] It was at this time that Joyce discovered, by receiving a letter of profuse gratitude from Joe's aged father in Amsterdam and thanking him for the efforts on behalf of the 'black sheep of my family,' that Joe was in reality the son of a well-known gynaecologist in a large European city. From prison Joe-Jules-Judas was transferred to the hospital. 'This time I am all in,' he wrote to Joyce. But he wasn't. For a brief period he acted as prompter for the English players. Then he disappeared. Six years or so later Joyce ran across him in Ostend. He was in good health, well-dressed and the owner of a large motorcar and a house in Brussels. And from there he disappears of Joyce's life. Rumour, however, has it that he has reformed and is now a pillar of respectability. (Herbert Gorman, *James Joyce*, New York, Rinehart & Company, 1948, pp. 243-245.)

Footnotes

Letters: Letters of James Joyce, edited by Stuart Gilbert, 1957, London, Faber and Faber (3 volumes)
Letters to Sylvia Beach: James Joyce, *Letters to Sylvia Beach 1921-1940*, edited by Melissa Banta and Oscar A. Silverman, Indiana University Press, 1987
CW: The Complete Works of James Joyce: Novels, Short Stories, Plays, Poetry, Essays & Letters, e-artnow, 2016 (e-book)

1. *CW*: 30 - 81-82/100.
2. *La Saison d'Ostende et du Littoral*, 50th year, no. 17, 8 August 1926, pp. 1-2.
3. *Letters to Sylvia Beach*, no. 79, p. 67.
4. *Letters to Sylvia Beach*, no. 80, p. 68.
5. Jonathan McCreedy, 'Everybody for Oneself but Code for us all', *Genetic Joyce Studies*, issue 10, Spring 2010.
6. Jean-Marie Bekaert, 'Albert Bouchery (1858-1941)', *De Plate* (Ostend), year 23, no. 1, January 1994, pp. 8-12.
7. *Letters*, I, p. 244.
8. Website: www.rootsireland.ie.
9. National Library of Ireland, call number MS 13,961/1/11.
10. Dublin, National Library of Ireland, call number LO 4406.
11. Information given by the National Library of Ireland, Dublin.
12. James Joyce Collection, University Libraries, University at Buffalo, State University of New York, inv. no. PCMS-0020.
13. London, British Library, ms 57348_f144v.
14. For the meaning and use of Joyce's sigla, see supra.
15. See David Hayman, 'Tristan and Isolde in *Finnegans Wake*: A Study of the Sources and Evolution of a Theme', *Comparative Literature Studies*, vol. 1, no. 2, 1964, pp. 93-112; Charles Long, '*Finnegans Wake*: Some Strange Tristan Influences', *Canadian Journal of Irish Studies*, vol. 15, no. 1, July 1989, pp. 23-33.
16. *Letters*, I, pp. 243-244.
17. Website Eishiro Into, T*he Japanese Elements of Finnegans Wake*: p-www.iwate-pu.ac.jp.
18. Website Wikipedia.
19. Website The James Joyce Centre, Dublin: www.jamesjoyce.ie.

20. R. F. Foster, *W.B. Yeats: A Life. I: The Apprentice Mage 1865-1914*, Oxford & New York, Oxford University Press, 1998, note 100 & note 102.

21. Robert Scholes & Richard M. Kain, *The Workshop of Daedalus. James Joyce and the Raw Materials for 'A Portrait of the Artist as a Young Man'*, Evanston (Ill.), Northwestern University Press, 1965, p. 73.

22. Website: www.annotatedshero.blogspot.be.

23. Website: www.jbhall.freeservers.com. The history of the church may be found in *Church of the Immaculate Conception Centenary Celebration 1892-1992* by Eddie Filgate, Tempest Dundalk, published in 1992.

24. Vincent Dean, Daniel Ferret, Geert Lernout, *James Joyce*. The Finnegans Wake *Notebooks at Buffalo*, Turnhout (Belgium), Brepols Publishers, 2001-2002.

25. Geert Lernout, *How Joyce wrote Finnegans Wake. A Chapter-by-chapter Genetic Guide* (Chapter One: The Beginning), The University of Wisconsin Press, 2007 [online].

26. *Letters*, III, pp. 256-257.

27. *Letters*, III, p. 257, note 1.

28. *The Irish Times*, 26 May 2012.

29. *Letters*, II, p. 244, note 10.

30. The Huntington Library (San Marino, CA) acquired the Frank Fay to Patrick Hoey letters from the Irish poet Austin Clarke (1896-1974) on 12 September 1962. The collection is also mentioned in a list of recent acquisitions in the November 1962 issue of the *Huntington Library Quarterly*.

31. Huntington Library, San Marino, California; inv. no. HM 26368.

32. Huntington Library, San Marino, California; inv. no. HM 26369.

33. Richard Ellmann, *James Joyce*, New York, Oxford University, 1959, pp. 166-167.

34. *Op. cit.*, p. 587.

35. *Letters*, I, pp. 244-245 [P.S. is missing]; *Letters to Sylvia Beach*, no. 81, pp. 68-69.

36. Ronan Crowley, 'Dial M for Marianne Moore. The *Dial's* Refusals of 'Work in Progress', *Genetic Joyce Studies*, Issue 15, Spring 2015.

37. Geert Lernout and Wim Van Mierlo, *The Reception of James Joyce in Europe*, 2004, p. 499.

38. Website: www.traditioninaction.org.

39. Richard Ellmann, *James Joyce*, New York, Oxford University Press, 1959, p. 592. Ellmann did not mention where he obtained this

information. It is not known what prompted this fleeting visit. Several of Lucia Joyce's photographs were almost certainly taken at Ostend airport on the same day (see Album of photographs, plates XI-XIII).

40. *Letters to Sylvia Beach*, no. 81, p. 69.
41. Website: Wikipedia.
42. *Letters*, III, pp. 141-142.
43. *Letters to Sylvia Beach*, no. 82, p. 69.
44. Ronan Crowley, 'Dial M for Marianne Moore. The Dial's Refusals of "Work in Progress"', *Genetic Joyce Studies*, Issue 15, Spring 2015.
45. Archives Valery Larbaud, Fonds patrimoniaux, Médiathèque Valery Larbaud, Vichy, France.
46. Website The James Joyce Centre, Dublin: www.jamesjoyce.ie.
47. Geert Lernout, *How Joyce wrote* Finnegans Wake. *A Chapter-by-chapter Genetic Guide*, The University of Wisconsin, 2007 [online].
48. Collection Hans E. Jahnke Bequest at the Zurich James Joyce Foundation, online at the National Library of Ireland, 2014 [JBZJJF/L/1/02].
49. London, British Library, ms. 57348_f150r.
50. *Letters to Sylvia Beach*, no. 83, pp. 69-70.
51. James Joyce Collection, University Libraries, University at Buffalo, State University of New York, inv. no. PCMS-0020. See annexe I.
52. CW: 20/64.
53. *Letters to Sylvia Beach*, no. 84, pp. 70-71. For more details concerning the manuscript, see Annexe I.
54. For the sigla, see supra.
55. Ronan Crowley, 'Dial M for Marianne Moore. The *Dial's* Refusals of "Work in Progress"', *Genetic Joyce Studies*, Issue 15, Spring 2015.
56. Website: www.erinoconnor.org.
57. Website The James Joyce Centre, Dublin: www.jamesjoyce.ie; information about Walsh posted by Dave Miller on website Flickr.
58. *Letters to Sylvia Beach*, p. 71.
59. *Letters*, p. 250; CW, pp. 28-29.
60. For the letters by Juda de Vries to James Joyce, see Annexe II.
61. Richard Ellmann, *James Joyce*, New York, Oxford University Press, 1959, p. 423.
62. Peter Spielberg, *James Joyce's Manuscripts & Letters at the University of Buffalo*, 1962, p. 164. Notebook VIII.A.5.
63. Website Bruce Stewart: www.ricorso.net.

64. Frank Budgen, *James Joyce and the Making of 'Ulysses' and other writings*, Oxford University Press, 1972, p. 29.

65. *Letters*, III, p. 426; CW: 3/51.

66. *Letters*, III, p. 426, note 7.

67. Herbert Gorman, *James Joyce*, New York, Rinehart & Company, 1948, pp. 243-245.

68. James Joyce, *Finnegans Wake*, with an introduction by Seamus Deane, London, Penguin Books, 1992, p. 287.

69. *Ibid.*, p. 502

70. *Ibid.*, p. 135.

ALBUM OF PHOTOGRAPHS

Photographs taken in Ostend in August-September 1926
(James Joyce Collection, the State University of New York, Buffalo)

The James Joyce Collection of the State University of New York in Buffalo owns a series of photographs showing the members of the Joyce family in Ostend in 1926. They were taken during two distinct periods during the months of August and September.

In his letter dated 2 September 1926 to Sylvia Beach, Joyce asks if she has received the 'snapshots' sent by Lucia. Joyce's letter enables us to pinpoint, with relative accuracy, the dates of the photographs. As the letter is dated 2 September and we know that James, Nora and Lucia Joyce arrived in Ostend on 5 or 6 August, the pictures must have been taken between 6 and 31 August. Taking into account the time needed to develop the negatives, we can narrow the period down further to 6 and 26 August. Since Lucia sent the photographs personally to Sylvia Beach, it is fair to assume that she was the main photographer. Joyce, who had bad eyesight, is pictured wearing an eye patch in the photographs. It seems unlikely, therefore, that he would have used the camera. The photographs showing Lucia, therefore, were probably taken by Nora. On Monday 16 August, a heavy thunderstorm passed over Ostend. Given that the Joyce family are unlikely to have walked around the city in such bad weather, we can assume that the photographs were taken between 6 and 15 August or 17 and 26 August. A number of photographs also include Giorgio Joyce. In his letter written in Italian on 1 September 1926, Joyce invites his son to join the family in Ostend. Allowing for the fact that the letter would have taken at least two days to reach Paris and that Giorgio needed to leave work and travel to the Belgian coast, we may assume that he arrived, at the earliest, around 4 September. As the Joyce family left Ostend for Ghent on 13 September, these particular photographs were probably taken between 5 and 12 September.

inv. no. 4.2
Nora Joyce (?): *Lucia Joyce standing on a breakwater at Ostend*, dated between 6 and 26 August 1926 [On the back of the photograph the stamp of the library Shakespeare & Co., Paris].

inv. no. 4.5

Nora Joyce (?): *Lucia Joyce with hat (Ostend)*, dated between 6 and 26 August 1926 [On the back of the photograph in Lucia Joyce's handwriting: *I am not wearing the | latest fashion hat as you | may think but simply | a 'sac à papier'! | Lucia.*' Lucia Joyce is not wearing a 'sac à papier' (paper bag) but a 'panier à papier' (paper basket)].

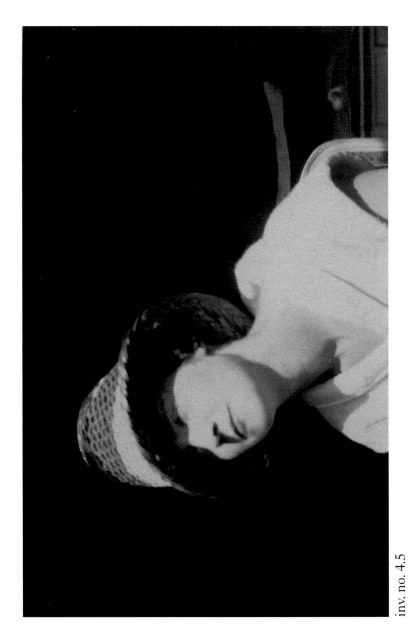

inv. no. 4.6

Nora Joyce (?): *Lucia Joyce seated at a table on a hotel terrace at Ostend*, dated between 6 and 26 August 1926 (A detail of this photograph is reproduced in Richard Ellmann, *James Joyce*, New York, Oxford University Press, 1959, pl. XVI, lower left, with the legend: 'Lucia Joyce. Courtesy of the Yale University Library').

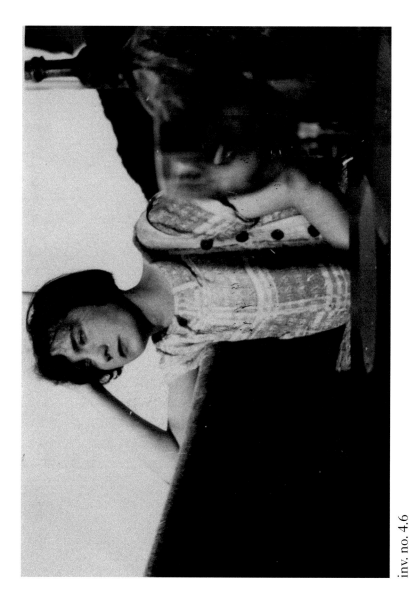

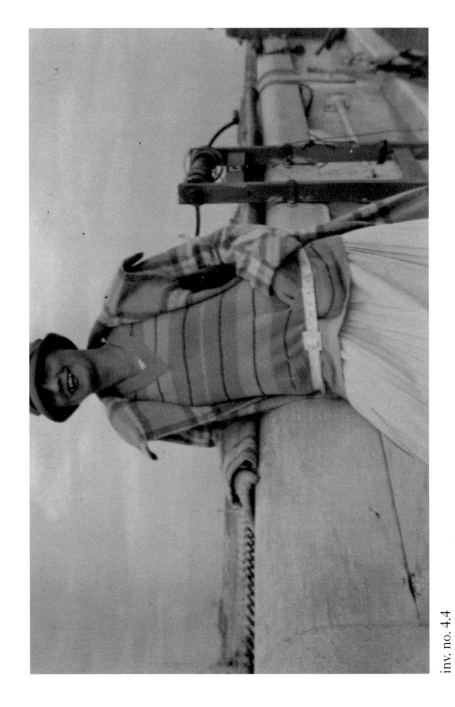

inv. no. 4.4
Nora Joyce (?): *Lucia Joyce on the pier at Ostend*, dated between 6 and 26 August 1926.

inv. no. 4.14

Lucia Joyce (?): Nora Joyce sitting in her room of the Hôtel de l'Océan at Ostend, dated between 6 and 26 August 1926.

inv. no. 4.10
Lucia Joyce (?): *Nora Joyce sitting on the steps of a beach cabin at Ostend*, dated between 6 and 26 August 1926.

inv. no. 4.15

Lucia Joyce (?): *Nora Joyce sitting on the beach at Ostend*, dated between 6 and 26 August 1926.

inv. no. 4.11

Lucia Joyce (?): *Nora Joyce sitting on a bench on the Promenade at Ostend*, dated between 6 and 26 August 1926.

inv. no. 4.3

Nora Joyce (?): *Lucia Joyce lying on the grass at Ostend*, dated between 6 and 26 August 1926 (probably around 26 August). [photograph taken the same day as 4.9].

inv. no. 4.9
Lucia Joyce (?): *James and Nora Joyce, with Patrick J. Hoey, lying on the grass at Ostend*, dated between 6 and 26 August 1926 (probably around 26 August). [photograph taken the same day as 4.3].

inv. no. 4.13
Lucia Joyce (?): *Nora Joyce near a British airplane, on the airfield at Ostend,*
taken probably on 26 August 1926 [photograph taken the same day as 4.7
and 4.8].

inv. no. 4.8

Lucia Joyce (?): *Group of people near a British airplane, on the airfield at Ostend*, taken probably on 26 August 1926 [photograph taken the same day as 4.7 and 4.13].

inv. no. 4.7

Lucia Joyce (?): *Airplane landing on the airfield of Ostend*, taken probably on 26 August 1926. [photograph taken the same day as 4.8 and 4.13].

inv. no. 4.16

Lucia Joyce (?): *James, Nora and Giorgio Joyce at a dining table in the park at Ostend,* dated between 5 and 12 September 1926 [taken the same day as 4.17 and 4.20] (This photograph was previously reproduced in *Letters of James Joyce,* volume III, edited by Richard Ellmann, London, Faber and Faber, 1966, not pag., with the following legend: *'Joyce, Mrs Joyce, and George at a restaurant, early 1920's*).

inv. no. 4.17

Lucia Joyce (?): *Nora and Giorgio Joyce at a dining table in the park at Ostend*, dated between 5 and 12 September 1926 [taken the same day as 4.16 and 4.20].

inv. no. 4.12
Lucia Joyce (?): *Nora Joyce in the park at Ostend*, between 5 and
12 September 1926.

inv. no 4.20
Lucia Joyce (?): *Giorgio Joyce on the Promenade at Ostend*, dated between 5
and 12 September 1926 [probably taken the same day as 4.16 and 4.17].

INDEX OF NAMES

Colophon

Publisher: Pandora Publishers
info@pandorapublishers.eu
Author: Xavier Tricot, Ostend
xavier.tricot@skynet.be
Cover design: Thomas Soete
www.thomassoete.com

The eight postcards and photographs of
Ostend, reproduced between p. 16 and p. 17,
come from the Beeldbank Kusterfgoed
(Image Bank – Coast Heritage).

© Pandora Publishers
and the author for his text

ISBN 9789053254684
W.D. 2020/5890/3